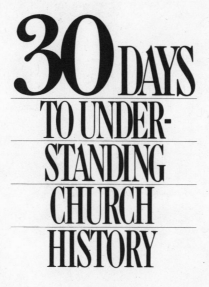

30 DAYS
TO UNDER-STANDING
CHURCH
HISTORY

30 DAYS TO UNDER-STANDING CHURCH HISTORY

Max E. Anders & Judith A. Lunsford

Wolgemuth & Hyatt, Publishers, Inc.
Brentwood, Tennessee

The mission of Wolgemuth & Hyatt, Publishers, Inc. is to publish and distribute books that lead individuals toward:

• A personal faith in the one true God: Father, Son, and Holy Spirit;

• A lifestyle of practical discipleship; and

• A worldview that is consistent with the historic, Christian faith.

Moreover, the Company endeavors to accomplish this mission at a reasonable profit and in a manner which glorifies God and serves His Kingdom.

Unless otherwise noted, all Scripture quotations are from the New American Standard Bible, ©1960, 1962, 1963, 1968, 1971, 1972, 1973, 1975, 1977, by The Lockman Foundation and are used by permission.

Wolgemuth & Hyatt, Publishers, Inc.
1749 Mallory Lane, Suite 110
Brentwood, Tennessee 37027

Library of Congress Cataloging-in-Publication Data

Anders, Max E., 1947–
   30 days to understanding church history / Max E. Anders, Judith A.
Lunsford.
      p. cm.
   Includes bibliographical references and index.
   ISBN 1-56121-084-6
   1. Church history—Popular works. I. Lunsford, Judith A.
II. Title. III. Title: Thirty days to understanding church history.
BR150.A53 1991
270—dc20   91-25380
                                            CIP

270 A53

In memory of
Bob Cleveland
who loved learning

CONTENTS

ACKNOWLEDGMENTS

T he authors would like to thank Mike Hyatt, whose vision brought church history into the 30 Days format. Special thanks go to Karen Moss and Shari Willman who contributed to the artwork.

PREFACE

Books with titles like *30 Days to Understanding* . . . are sometimes perceived as literary marshmallows, not works of substance. However, the "30 Days" series on which I have embarked, having written *30 Days to Understanding the Bible* and *30 Days to Understanding the Christian Life,* are not literary marshmallows flung in a party atmosphere to the Christian public to *enjoy* but not to *nourish*. Rather they are books rooted in a deep conviction that most learning is self-generated. Because of this, we must teach the basics and teach them well. When a person learns the basics well, he is then positioned to go on to self-directed advanced learning. Therefore, when laying the foundation of any body of learning, teaching *less* is teaching *more*. These books, and others that I hope to do in the future, are expressions of a very deeply held philosophy of ministry and education. They are rooted in many years of study and teaching.

The need for these kinds of books transcends my own areas of expertise, and it has come like a breath of fresh air to discover that a long-time friend of mine, Judy Lunsford, is a kindred spirit. She, too, has a deep conviction about the value of putting survey information into a creative format and enticing people to learn. With that conviction, she brings a tremendous insight and skill into the art of teaching less, in order to teach more.

Judy is the "church history brains" behind this book. Her prodigious research and considerable skill make her the major contributor to this work, and she rightly deserves the lion's share of the credit for it. I have a passion for the "30 Days" idea and have come along to offer whatever expertise I could in the area of methodology.

I can't tell you how much I have learned about church history myself. Unless you are already a student of church history, you will learn more than you expected. You will appreciate our spiritual heritage more than ever before. You will be enriched by seeing the drama of Christ's church unfolding through the ages. And, even if you are a student of church history already, you will probably come away with a clearer vision of the big picture than ever before.

We offer you this book from the depths of our hearts and the substance of our minds, in the sincere hope that you will both enjoy and profit from a greater historical understanding of this great mystery, the Bride of Christ, the church.

MAX E. ANDERS
Austin, Texas
A.D. 1991

INTRODUCTION

T he statistics are mind-boggling: one-third of the world's 5.3 billion people are Christians, including 963 million Roman Catholics, 324 million Protestants, 180 million Eastern Orthodox, and 54 million Anglicans.

Who are these people? Why are they labeled Christian *and* Roman Catholic, Christian *and* Protestant, Christian *and* Eastern Orthodox, and Christian *and* Anglican? What do they believe? When did they get started? Who were their spokesmen?

What we need is a good, readable book on church history.

But, wait a minute. My office bulges with books. Right now fifty books line my worktable—short squatty paperbacks and colossal tomes. Most of them are history books, and the vast majority cover church history. They are fine books, well-written and well-researched. If you read these books, you will find the answers to your questions and, in the process, become a church historian.

The problem is that most of us don't want to become church historians. We want to become informed Christians. How do we become informed without being overwhelmed by the subject? *30 Days To Understanding Church History* is the place to begin.

30 Days To Understanding Church History is a primer that provides a comprehensive overview of Christianity quickly and painlessly. The book looks like other history books and contains facts like other history books, but *30 Days To Understanding Church History* does more than impart knowledge. Using a simple teaching technique, *30 Days To Understanding Church History* helps the reader organize information, integrate ideas, and remember what he has learned.

In fact, if you will invest fifteen minutes of your time each day for thirty days, you will become familiar with many aspects of the church:

- its geography
- its major periods and eras
- its concepts and foes
- its key figures
- its writers and writings
- its general trends

At the end of one month, you will understand the ebb and flow of church history, and your understanding will form a sturdy superstructure on which to hang other historical facts. In addition, you will become thoroughly acquainted with a book that can be used repeatedly as a reference tool.

30 Days To Understanding Church History will not make you a church historian. It will, however, give you an informed understanding of Christianity, an appreciation for the post-biblical heroes of the faith, and, best of all, a great sense of accomplishment. *30 Days To Understanding Church History* may inspire you to delve more deeply into your own Christian heritage. Who knows? You may want to pick up one of those squatty paperbacks or colossal tomes!

Enjoy the adventure ahead.

FOUNDATIONAL MATERIAL

ONE

TIME AND HISTORY

With a dynamic present and an uncertain future, who has time for the Greeks and Romans? Frequently, our reactions to history parallel the feelings expressed in Arthur Guiterman's poem, *Ancient History:*

> I hope the old Romans
> Had painful abdomens.
>
> I hope that the Greeks
> Had toothache for weeks.
>
> I hope the Egyptians
> Had chronic conniptions.
>
> I hope that the Arabs
> Were bitten by scarabs.
>
> I hope that the Persians
> Had gout in all versions.
>
> I hope that the Medes
> Were kicked by their steeds.
>
> They started the fuss
> And left it to us![1]

Still, we can't dismiss history too quickly because we know that every custom and institution that affects life today is a product of history, and deep down, we know we should understand more than we do.

Most of us define *history* as "anything that happened before we were born." It's a useful definition because, to one degree or another, during our lifetimes we sort through the things that happened before we were born.

Our problem with history comes when our sorting gets bogged down. We get stuck in dates and battles, mired in causes and effects, and stymied by customs and names.

Things become even more confused when we focus on something off-beat, like church history. We wrestle with concepts. What is *secular*? What is *sacred*? Where do church leaders fit into real history?

We acknowledge the dilemma: How do we devote ourselves to understanding the past and still have time for the present?

The poem, "Ancient History," provides some help. If we look carefully, we will see that the amusing curses are actually aimed at specific groups of people: the Romans, Greeks, Egyptians, etc.— the VIPs of the ancient world.

If we arrange the information on paper, it might look like:

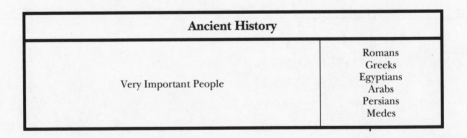

Ancient History	
Very Important People	Romans Greeks Egyptians Arabs Persians Medes

There is a lesson to learn: dividing information helps us sort history into manageable units.

The lesson bears repeating: *dividing information helps us sort history into manageable units.*

Time

During the 1500s, historians began using the special term, *period,* to describe time. A period was an interval during which a cycle or series of events moved toward a conclusion. One period followed another. If consecutive periods were mentioned in a series, they were listed chronologically—the earliest period was mentioned first, while the most recent was mentioned last.

The history of Western civilization is a good illustration. It has three periods: the Ancient Period, the Medieval Period, and the Modern Period. The Ancient Period was the earliest and is mentioned first. The Modern Period is the latest and is noted last.

If we were to organize this information on paper, it would look like this:

History	
Time Periods of Western Civilization	Ancient Period Medieval Period Modern Period

Each of the three periods of Western civilization has different characteristics. The Ancient Period bustled with activity, most of which centered around the Mediterranean Sea. (We need to remind ourselves that *ancient* does not mean dull!) Engineers built wonders—the pyramids and the Hanging Gardens. Warrior kings, like Nebuchadnezzar, Alexander, and the Caesars, managed empires. There were philosophers and poets. The Ancient Period includes everything that happened up to A.D. 476, the "fall" of the Roman Empire.

The Medieval Period sometimes confuses us, not because we can't understand what happened, but because the Medieval Period is identified by several names. One of its aliases is the Middle Ages. Since *medieval* literally means "the middle age," the terms *Medieval Period* and *the Middle Ages* are used interchangeably.

The Dark Ages adds to our confusion. The Dark Ages began with the barbarians and ended around 1000. So, the Dark Ages refers only to a portion of the Middle Ages.

Most medieval activity focused on Europe. It was a time of unrest, instability, and plagues. Society was decentralized, rural. There was little advance in learning. The feudal system, with its castles and knights, sought to keep order but often created chaos. The order imposed by the church stabilized the Western world, and seeds were sown which blossomed later as cities revived, universities were founded, modern languages evolved, and national states developed.

The Modern Period of Western civilization began with worldwide exploration and continues through today. The conquistadors built empires and searched for natural resources. Commerce flourished. Education advanced. Nations matured. Wars were waged. People began to understand science and develop technology.

As we have looked at these time periods, something interesting has occurred. Because we first sorted history into meaningful and manageable units, the information we have just discussed is easily absorbed.

SUMMARY

The three time divisions of Western civilization are the Ancient Period, the Medieval Period, and the Modern Period.

_____ focused on the Mediterranean area.
_____ concentrated on Europe.
_____ saw worldwide exploration.

History

The periods—the Ancient Period, the Medieval Period, and the Modern Period—when looked at together, form an arc over the history of Western civilization.

Arc of Western History

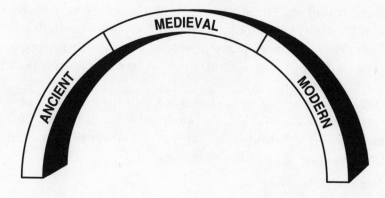

Once we understand the Arc of Western History, we are better equipped to deal with details. The dates, battles, and peculiar customs, which once confused us, can now be filed under one of these major time categories. We can think of the history of Western civilization as a three-drawer filing cabinet with the drawers labeled Ancient, Medieval, and Modern. When a new fact confronts us, we merely open the correct drawer and toss it in.

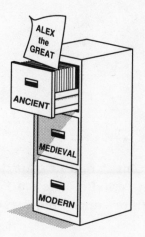

This organizing technique works well for the history of Western civilization, but will it work for church history?

Church history traces the development of Christianity from its infancy around A.D. 30 through our modern day. Like the progression of Western civilization, the church has passed through distinct periods. What surprises many people is that church history parallels the history of Western civilization. In fact, Christianity fathered Western civilization.

Church history can also be divided into three distinct periods: the Ancient Church Period, the Medieval Church Period, and the Modern Church Period. Like the Arc of Western History, these periods form an Arc of Church History.

Arc of Church History

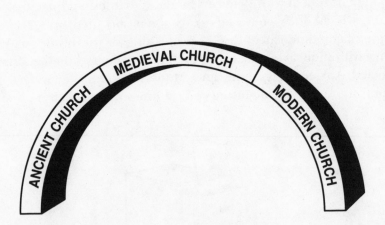

Although the Ancient Period of Church history began much later than the Ancient Period of Western Civilization, we can slip the Arc of Church History under the Arc of Western History to show the effect.

Arc of Church History
Joins the Arc of Western History

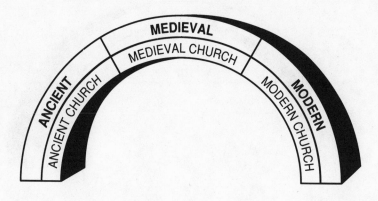

The successive periods in church history form consecutive time spans. The Ancient Church began about A.D. 30 and continued through the final collapse of the Roman Empire, about 600. The Medieval Church spanned the years 600–1550. The Modern Church began about 1550.

SUMMARY

Church history falls into three distinct periods:

the _____ (A.D. 30–600),
the _____ (600–1550), and
the _____ (1550 to the present).

Self-Test

To check your answers, see the previous pages.

A. Fill in the Arc of Western History.

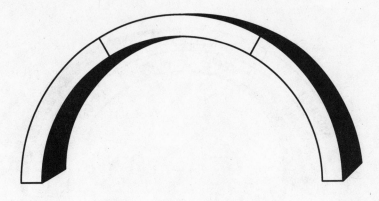

B. Fill in the Arc of Church History.

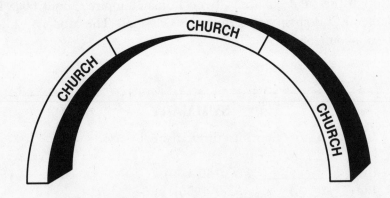

C. Match the following periods with their correct dates.

_____ Ancient Church   a. 1550–present

_____ Medieval Church   b. A.D. 30–600

_____ Modern Church   c. A.D. 600–1550

D. Date the periods of Church history on the spaces provided.

_____ The Ancient Church
_____ The Medieval Church
_____ The Modern Church

E. Fill in the blanks.

1. What are the three divisions in the history of Western civilization? _____, _____, and _____.

2. Which period came first? _____.

3. Which period came last? _____.

ᐖ   ᐖ   ᐖ

Congratulations! You have now begun the sorting process. You know the main periods of church history and their corresponding dates.

In the days ahead you will discover new details to slip under these periods. In less than a month you will gain a broad understanding of church history and a better understanding of the history of Western civilization. Best of all, because you will be sorting and using the information, you will remember what you have learned.

TWO

ERAS, EPOCHS, AND DATES

O ne day in the House of Commons, Winston Churchill was criticizing governmental policy. Referring to Prime Minister Stanley Baldwin, Churchill thundered, "History will say that the right honorable gentleman was wrong in this matter." After a moment, Churchill confided, "I know it will, because I shall write the history."[1]

Not all historians wrote with such a vengeance, but they did write from a particular point of view. Consider the great Greek historians, Herodotus (c. 484–c. 430 B.C.) and Thucydides (c. 460–c. 400 B.C.). Herodotus fathered history. His first best-seller was aptly called *History*, which came from the Greek word *histor*, meaning "learned man." Herodotus was a newsy, chatty, tell-it-like-it-is-taking-a-few-liberties war correspondent.

The younger Thucydides was a political scientist; he was critical, analytical, and probing. Thucydides hoped his history, *The Peloponnesian War*, "would be judged useful by those inquirers who desire an exact knowledge of the past as an aid to the interpretation of the future."

The styles of the two men illustrate the different ways writers package history. Some historians simply record events. We might call

15

their approach "objective journalism"; scholars call it *historiography*. Other writers look for meaning behind the facts and interpret the events they record. Our study of church history borrows from both approaches.

About a hundred years after historians introduced the term *period,* they added two other important words: *era* and *epoch.* Let's look at each word separately.

Eras

An era is a duration of time marked by a new or distinct order of things. Each period of church history—the Ancient Church, the Medieval Church, the Modern Church—can be divided into two descriptive eras. As we look at these six eras of church history, we will assign a title and a symbol to each.

The Ancient Church Period

The Ancient Church Period covered two distinct eras:

1. The Infant Church Era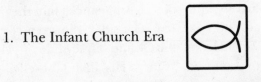

2. The Adolescent Church Era

The titles of the eras from the Ancient Church Period parallel human development and help us remember what happened to the church. The Infant Church experienced great growth; the Adolescent Church struggled for its identity.

Since we know that dividing information helps us sort history into manageable units, let's add the information about the eras to the Arc of Church History.

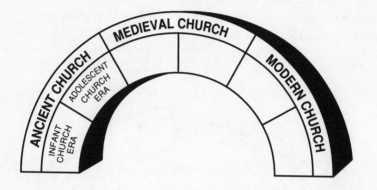

SUMMARY

The Ancient Church Period had two eras:

the_____ Church Era and

the_____ Church Era.

The Medieval Church Period

The Medieval Church Period covered two distinct eras:

1. The Roman Church Era

2. The Reformation Church Era

The Roman Church coped with the barbarians and struggled to maintain order. The Reformation Church pushed for changes in ecclesiastical policies and practices. Let's add these two eras to our Arc of Church History.

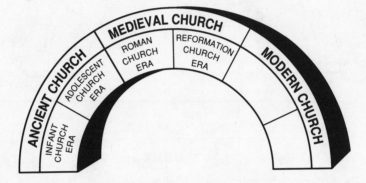

SUMMARY

The Medieval Church Period had two eras:

the_____ Church Era and

the_____ Church Era.

The Modern Church Period

The Modern Church Period covered two distinct eras:

1. The Denominational Church Era

2. The Global Church Era

The Denominational Church saw Christians splinter into distinct corporate bodies. The Global Church used technology to spread Christianity throughout the world.

Let's add these two recent eras to our Arc of Church History.

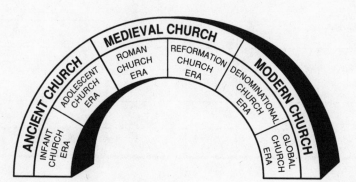

SUMMARY

The Modern Church Period had two eras:

the_____ Church Era and

the_____ Church Era.

Tacitus wrote, "This I regard as history's highest function, to let no worthy action go uncommemorated." However, in A.D. 100, Tacitus had fewer actions to remember than we do today. How do we manage the avalanche of events that has occurred since the church began? We continue dividing and sorting information, highlighting only the major events. A chart will help us by providing a framework on which to hang smaller details.

We know the three periods of church history. Let's arrange them chronologically on our chart:

Period	Era	Date	Epoch	Pivotal Church Figure	Story Line
Ancient Church					
Medieval Church					
Modern Church					

Since we also know the six eras of church history, we can add them to our chart.

Period	Era	Date	Epoch	Pivotal Church Figure	Story Line
Ancient Church	Infant				
	Adolescent				
Medieval Church	Roman				
	Reformation				
Modern Church	Denominational				
	Global				

Now we are ready to look closely at some of history's "worthy actions."

Epochs

In addition to the term *era,* historians use the word *epoch.* An epoch is a date or event that turns the course of history. An epoch kicks off an era. In 1928, for instance, the animated film *Mickey Mouse* ushered in an new era in the movie industry.

Epochs are important. If we recognize the epoch of an era, we have a good idea of what occurred during that era. Let's look at the epochs in church history. (Each epoch appears in bold italic type.)

The Ancient Church Period

Infant Church Era: The Infant Church began with the coming of the Holy Spirit on Pentecost. ***Pentecost Sunday*** marked the beginning of church history.

Adolescent Church Era: The Adolescent Church matured as ***Constantine,*** the Roman emperor, favored Christianity, gave it celebrity status, and encouraged it to develop distinct practices and policies.

SUMMARY

The epoch for the Infant Church Era was _____.

The epoch for the Adolescent Church Era was
the reign of _____.

The Medieval Church Period

Roman Church Era: The Roman Church struggled with the chaos of the barbarians until ***Gregory the Great,*** the bishop of Rome, stepped in.

Reformation Church Era: The *Renaissance* exalted man's abilities, rekindled an interest in ancient Greek and Roman cultures, and encouraged man to value his relationship with his world above his relationship with God. The Reformation Church responded to this new thinking.

SUMMARY

The epoch for the Roman Church Era was the leadership of _____.

The epoch for the Reformation Church Era was the _____.

The Modern Church Period

Denominational Church Era: The *Council of Trent,* the official response to the growing calls for reform, redefined the foundational precepts of Catholic belief and ended hope for a Protestant-Catholic reconciliation.

Global Church Era: The *French Revolution* created a world tossed about by powerful political ideas and heralded the beginning of the Global Church Era.

SUMMARY

The epoch for the Denominational Church Era was the _____.

The epoch for the Global Church Era was the _____.

Dates

Now that we have connected the eras with their epochs, we can easily add some dates. We look at the date on which an epoch occurred and stretch the time for its era to the next epoch. (Each set of dates appears in bold italic type.)

The Ancient Church Period

Infant Church Era: The Infant Church Era began on Pentecost Sunday around *A.D. 30* and continued until the next epoch, the reign of Constantine, around *325.*

Adolescent Church Era: The Adolescent Church Era began with Constantine around *325* and continued until Gregory the Great became bishop of Rome around *600.*

SUMMARY

The Ancient Church Period with its two eras roughly extends from A.D. 30–600.

The time span of the _____ Church Era is A.D. 30–325.

The time span of the _____ Church Era is A.D. 325–600.

The Medieval Church Period

Roman Church Era: The Roman Church Era began with Gregory the Great around *600* and continued until the Renaissance in *1300.*

Reformation Church Era: The Reformation Church Era began with the Renaissance around *1300* and continued until the Council of Trent around *1550.*

SUMMARY

The Medieval Church Period with its two eras extends from 600–1550.

The time span of the _____ Church Era is 600–1300.

The time span of the _____ Church Era is 1300–1550.

The Modern Church Period

Denominational Church Era: The Denominational Church Era began with the Council of Trent around *1550* and stretched until the French Revolution in *1789.*

Global Church Era: The Global Church Era began with the French Revolution in *1789* and continues into the present.

SUMMARY

The Modern Church Period with its two eras began around 1550 and extends into the present.

The time span of the _____ Church Era is 1550–1789.

The time span of the _____ Church Era is 1789–present.

Self-Test

To check your answers, see previous pages.

A. Place the correct epoch on the chart below.

Council of Trent   Gregory the Great   Constantine
Renaissance   Pentecost Sunday   French Revolution

Era	Epoch
Infant Church	
Adolescent Church	
Roman Church	
Reformation Church	
Denominational Church	
Global Church	

B. Place the following time spans next to their correct eras.

1550–1789   1300–1550   325–600
1789–present   600–1300   30–325

Era	Date
Infant Church	
Adolescent Church	
Roman Church	
Reformation Church	
Denominational Church	
Global Church	

C. Fill in the missing items on the chart below.

Period	Era	Date	Epoch	Pivotal Church Figure	Story Line
Ancient Church	Infant				
		325–600			
Medieval Church					
	Reformation				
Modern Church					
			French Revolution		

ta   ta   ta

Congratulations! You have just completed one of the pivotal chapters in *30 Days to Understanding Church History*. From this point on you will add information in smaller bites.

About the Symbols

Ichthus—The ichthus (fish) was the earliest Christian symbol. The Greek word for fish (ΙΧΘΥΣ) also formed a five-letter Greek anagram that contained the first letters of the phrase "Jesus Christ Son of God Savior." The ichthus symbol was used to test strangers. A Christian would draw an arc on the ground. If the stranger was a Christian, he would complete the figure.

Chi-Rho—The Chi-Rho was a monogram formed by the first two letters (X = Chi and P = Rho) of the Greek word for Christ. The symbol was a favorite of Constantine, who made it the insignia of the military during the Adolescent Church Era.

Miter—A miter was a tall headpiece that was worn during the Roman Church Era. The miter, a symbol of authority, was first used during the Middle Ages by the highest officials of the church.

Open Bible—The open Bible was a medieval symbol of rule. During the Reformation Church Era there was a persistent cry to return to Scripture as the basis for authority and church practices.

Arrows—During the Denominational Church Era, Christianity splintered into three traditions—Orthodoxy, Catholicism, and Protestantism—and Protestantism underwent further fragmentation.

Globe—In medieval art, the globe was a symbol of power. This symbol was chosen for the Global Church Era to illustrate the worldwide spread of Christianity during the nineteenth and twentieth centuries.

THREE

PIVOTAL CHURCH FIGURES

T he words *mosque, temple, church,* and *synagogue* identify places of worship and suggest religious affiliations. Muslims worship in mosques. Hindus pray at a temple. Christians have churches, and Jews go to the synagogue. Words can also describe people in religious leadership—rabbi, imam, and guru.

No history of the Christian church is complete without a look at its leadership. While we associate a priest, a pastor, or a minister with Christianity today, different kinds of leaders have shaped its development. In each of the six eras of church history there has been a dominant category of leadership that has nurtured, strengthened, guided, and protected the church. Let's identify the pivotal church figure for each era.

The Ancient Church Period

Infant Church Era (30–325)

During the first century, the apostles guided the young churches. As the apostles died, **bishops** replaced them. Although this shift in leadership was gradual, the guidelines for selecting bishops were already in place by A.D. 62–63, when two New Testament books, 1 Timothy and Titus, were written.

By A.D. 110, a three-tiered leadership structure was common among the churches in Asia Minor. The hierarchy consisted of a bishop, a body of elders, and several deacons. This structure spread steadily throughout the churches of the empire.

As the leading figure, the bishop did important work; he edified (instructed) the local church. His duties included:

- Teaching and preaching
- Conducting the Lord's Supper
- Advising other churches
- Settling disputes
- Reading, studying, and collecting New Testament writings
- Urging godliness and unity among believers

Adolescent Church Era (325–600)

Like a human adolescent, the church struggled to "grow up." The men who shaped the beliefs and gave identity to the Adolescent Church were the *theologians.*

Theologians were highly educated men who were familiar with the Scriptures, well versed in languages, understood philosophy, and were skilled writers.

Theologians devoted themselves to one or more of the following activities:

- Formulating doctrinal statements
- Correcting errors in teaching
- Developing preaching techniques
- Encouraging the monastic movement
- Training leaders

SUMMARY

_____ edified the Infant Church.

_____ shaped the beliefs of the Adolescent Church.

The Medieval Church Period

Roman Church Era (600–1300)

By the close of the Adolescent Church Era, the barbarians had turned society upside down. The Vandals were in North Africa; the Goths were in Spain. The Franks occupied France; the Lombards, Italy; the Angles and Saxons, England.

The task of civilizing the barbarians fell to the *monks* who lived among the unruly tribes. Monasteries, which originally had been isolated retreats for the Romans, became scattered islands of civilization.

Civilizing the barbarians was not easy. Many were pagans. Few understood the teachings of Jesus and had no intention of "turning the other cheek." Barbarians were belligerent and aggressive and tolerated Christianity only because it was the religion of the once-mighty Roman Empire.

Monks, in essence, transmitted or preserved the Christian and Greco-Roman cultures. They taught academics and practical skills—farming, engineering, baking, animal husbandry, and calligraphy. Monks occasionally left their monasteries to accept other positions within the church, but most remained attached to their monasteries and functioned creatively as educators, administrators, historians, teachers, and missionaries.

Reformation Church Era (1300–1550)

During the Middle Ages there was constant tension between the pope—the chief leader of the medieval church—and ruling monarchs. Both wanted control over society. As the popes gained the upper hand, they gradually added doctrines or practices to substantiate and solidify their position. Injustices and inconsistencies arose. By 1300, *reformers* within the church were openly questioning religious practices and teachings and calling for correction and improvement.

The reformers were students of the Bible who tried to:

- Use Scripture as the sole basis for authority
- Place Christ as the head of the church

- Translate the Bible into native languages
- Promote personal Bible reading
- Encourage a biblical life-style
- Foster financial accountability
- Abolish nonbiblical church practices

SUMMARY

_____ preserved culture and provided leadership during the Roman Church Era.

_____ urged the Reformation Church to return to a more biblical basis.

The Modern Church Period

Denominational Church Era (1550–1789)

The Council of Trent ended all hope for reforming the Roman church. The reforming "protesters" of the early sixteenth century became known as Protestants, and Christianity essentially divided into three traditions: the Eastern Orthodox church, the Roman Catholic church, and the Protestant church.

Among the Protestants there arose sharp differences of opinion over the ways to reform the church. These differences led to new controversies, new dogmas (teachings authoritatively proclaimed), and even greater division. Christian leaders became *churchmen* who advocated specific dogmas and practices.

For nearly one hundred years (1550–1650), *churchmen* settled the issues of doctrine, organization, and church-state relationships on the battlefields of Europe. When the smoke cleared, denominationalism had become a predominant characteristic of the modern church.

Global Church Era (1789–present)

In 1789, the Western world was rapidly changing. The American colonies had wrested independence from England. Common men grasped new ideals. Technology promised convenience. Factories and cities restructured life.

During this dynamic time, a new breed of church leadership emerged to address the spiritual, and often the physical, needs of people. This leadership functioned under names like *missionary, revivalist, evangelist,* and *linguist;* collectively, we will call them **strategists.** Strategists seized the opportunities presented by a changing society to present the gospel in unique, creative, and nontraditional ways. Many of the early strategists were laymen.

SUMMARY

_____ advocated specific dogmas and practices during the Denominational Church Era.

_____ from the Global Church Era presented the gospel and solved problems using innovation and emerging technology.

Self-Test

A. Write the pivotal church figure beside its correct description.

Churchmen   Theologians   Bishops
Monks   Strategists   Reformers

_____ Emphasized dogma and denominations.

_____ Sought a return to biblical standards.

_____ Tamed the barbarians.

_____ Clarified the beliefs of Christianity.

_____ Gently nurtured and edified the church.

_____ Presented the gospel using innovation and technology.

B. Match the era with its pivotal church figure.

_____ Infant Church   a. Churchmen

_____ Adolescent Church   b. Reformers

_____ Roman Church   c. Theologians

_____ Reformation Church   d. Strategists

_____ Denominational Church   e. Bishops

_____ Global Church   f. Monks

C. Fill in the Arc of Church History.

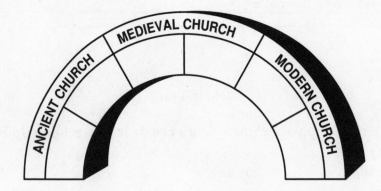

D. Fill in the Story of Church History.

Period	Era	Date	Epoch	Pivotal Church Figure	Story Line

❧   ❧   ❧

Tomorrow, let's narrow our focus to the Ancient Church Period.

THE ANCIENT CHURCH PERIOD

FOUR

GEOGRAPHY: ANCIENT CHURCH PERIOD

T he Ancient Church, birthed in a Roman world, was swaddled by a cosmopolitan society. Did you know that during the second century:

- A messenger could travel from Rome to Spain in thirty-six hours?
- A foreign slave was cheaper than a horse?
- The best doctors came from Alexandria?
- Gallic (early French) nobles were distinguished by their mustachios?
- Innkeepers customarily robbed their guests?
- The inhabitants of Rome annually consumed twenty-five million gallons of wine—two quarts per week for every man, woman, and child?
- A passenger could sail from Sicily to Alexandria in six days?
- Pork was the meat of choice?
- Rome used three hundred million gallons of water daily?

What have slaves and pork to do with church history?

Places, food, climate, and customs are the building blocks of geography, and geographical facts, like tiny muscle fibers, energize history. Understanding the significance of a single geographical fact often provides broad historical insight.

Take local customs. The Christians in Rome baffled their contemporaries. Lucian (c. 160) called them "imbeciles." Christians disdained material things, yet they burrowed under Rome, fashioning catacombs for corpses. To a Roman, this behavior was bizarre because Rome had no cemeteries; dead Romans were cremated.

Consider climate. Recall that Paul, a prisoner in Rome, prodded Timothy in Ephesus: "Make every effort to come before winter" (2 Timothy 4:21, NAS). This was no homesick longing. Paul was a veteran traveler on the Mediterranean. He had been shipwrecked four times! Paul knew that few ships sailed during the winter, November through March, because of seasonal storms. Paul's urging was based on simple geography.

As we examine the Ancient Church Period, we will focus on simple geography, and simple geography means maps. We will stick to the basics: bodies of water, Roman regions, and important cities.

The Infant Church Era

Bodies of Water

The anchor points in the geography of the Ancient Church Period are the bodies of water. As you read each description, write the name of the body of water beside the Roman numeral on the work map (see page 42).

- *The Mediterranean Sea* (I). The Ancient Church, like its contemporary, the Roman Empire, developed around the Mediterranean Sea.
- *The Aegean Sea* (II). The Aegean Sea is an arm of the Mediterranean Sea which separates Achaia, modern Greece, from Asia Minor, modern Turkey.

- *The Black Sea* (III). The Black Sea is a large, inland body of water located directly north of Asia Minor with an outlet into the Mediterranean Sea.

Regions

The important Roman provinces were located around the main bodies of water. As you read each description, write the name of the region beside the capital letter on the work map (see page 42).

- *Judea* (A). The Roman province of Judea was the cradle of Christianity.

- *Syria* (B). After the stoning of Stephen and the ensuing persecution, many converts fled to Syria, where colonies of Jews already flourished. Syria was on the trade route to China and India.

- *Asia Minor* (C). Asia Minor was the peninsula bounded by the Black Sea on the north, the Aegean on the west, and the Mediterranean on the south. Paul visited Asia Minor on all three of his missionary journeys. Asia Minor was one of the most thoroughly Christianized regions in the empire.

- *Macedonia and East Achaia* (D). Paul focused on the Roman provinces of Macedonia and Achaia during his second missionary journey. Both regions were located west of the Aegean Sea.

- *Italy* (E). Italy was the birthplace of the Roman Empire.

- *Gaul* (F). Gaul was the ancient name for the area northwest of Italy, the site of modern France and Belgium. Both Julius Caesar and the historian Ammianus Marcellinus described the Gauls as a tall, blond, muscular, and quarrelsome people who wore breeches and loved gold jewelry.[1]

- *Britain* (G). Although Julius Caesar invaded Britain in 53 B.C., when Herod the Great was twenty years old, Rome's actual conquest of Britain began in A.D. 43, two years before Paul began his first missionary journey. Little is known of how Christianity came to Britain, but a strong Christian Celtic church sent representatives to church councils as early as the fourth century.

- *Spain* (H). Slaves from all over the Empire were sent to Spain to mine lead, iron, tin, silver, copper, and gold. The country, home to two famous Roman emperors—Trajan and Hadrian, was also known for a spicy fish sauce called *garum*.

- **North Africa** (J). Christianity came early to North Africa and thrived until the Muslim invasions during the seventh century. North Africa was thoroughly Romanized and contained twelve retirement colonies for Roman soldiers.

- **Egypt** (K). Egypt was Rome's granary. In the delta area, Christianity was well established by the end of the first century.

Work map

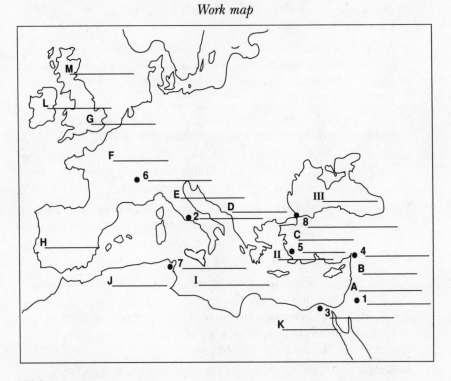

Cities

The Infant Church developed in the cities along the highways and seaports of the empire. As you read about each city, write its name beside the Arabic numeral on the work map.

- **Jerusalem** (1). War diminished the influence of Jerusalem on the Infant Church. In A.D. 66, Jewish Christians did not support a revolt against Rome; hundreds of Christians fled to Pella, a city east of the Jordan. In A.D. 70, Rome destroyed Jerusalem. As a result, the Jews charged the Christians with treason and banished them from their synagogues. After A.D. 70, few Jews became Christians, and Christians looked to Rome and Antioch for church leadership.

- **Rome** (2). Rome was the capital of the empire, with a second-century population numbering between 800,000 and 1.2 million. Half were slaves. Twenty thousand were Jews. The inhabitants resided on less than ten square miles of land and were remarkably rich or abysmally poor. Pools, gardens, and fine sculpture adorned the homes of the wealthy, but the working classes lived in tenements. Streets were noisy, dirty, and smelled of sewage. Rome, the city of the emperors and the seat of government, showcased splendid fountains, magnificent buildings, and a culture envied by the civilized world. By A.D. 100, Rome was the focal city of Christianity.

SUMMARY

_____ was the focal city of the Infant Church Era.

- **Alexandria** (3). Alexandria, an Egyptian city brimming with culture, was second only to Rome in importance. Alexandria had a Christian community in the first century and was famous for its school for baptismal candidates. Alexandria was the city where the *Septuagint*—the Greek version of the Old Testament that was used by the Infant Church—had been translated around 250 B.C.

- **Antioch** (4). Antioch, a military center and the capital of the Roman province of Syria, was the third most important city in the empire. From the city's founding, Jews had been granted citizenship and the right to own land. Around A.D. 31, Jewish Christians, fleeing persecution in Jerusalem, established the first church in Antioch. There, Paul and Barnabas taught; believers were first called Christians; and the first missionaries were commissioned.

- *Ephesus* (5). Ephesus, the capital of the Roman province of Asia in the region of Asia Minor, was a center of wealth, trade, commerce, and Roman religion. Even though it was the hub of the pagan religious world, the Infant Church made great inroads there. Paul taught in Ephesus, Timothy pastored there, and tradition teaches that it was the home city of the aging Apostle John.

- *Lyons* (6). Lyons, the principal city in Gaul, was founded in 43 B.C. as a Roman colony. The city exerted a strong influence on the Infant Church because Irenaeus, the bishop of Lyons, was the leading spokesman against gnosticism, a false teaching. In A.D. 177, the Christians of Lyons experienced a severe local persecution. Many, including a young slave girl named Blandina, were brutally tortured.

- *Carthage* (7). Carthage, older than Rome and one of its chief rivals, was the home of two of the most important Latin-speaking leaders in the Infant Church: the controversial writer Tertullian (c. 150–c. 212), and Cyprian (c. 200–258), the first bishop martyred in the North African churches. In Cyprian's day, the church at Carthage was wealthy and nearly as influential as the church at Rome.

The Adolescent Church Era

Under Constantine, new regions and cities became important. As you read each description, write the name of the important place in its appropriate location on the work map (see page 42).

Regions

- *Ireland* (L) *and Scotland* (M). Ireland and Scotland were not Roman provinces, but they were important regions during the Adolescent Church Era. Around 430, Patrick, a monk from the Celtic church in Britain, began to evangelize Ireland. A century later, Columba, another Celtic monk, reached Scotland. The Celtic church taught the Scriptures and emphasized evangelism, education, music, and the calligraphic reproduction of manuscripts.

Cities

- *Constantinople* (8). In 330, to counter the barbarian threat in the east, Constantine built a new capital for the empire near the strategic Black Sea and called it Constantinople. The city was initially home to about fifty thousand people. Its ruling class was primarily a Latin aristocracy. The focal point of "new Rome" was a church, the magnificent Hagia Sophia. Gradually, Constantinople, modern Istanbul, Turkey, became the premier city in the empire and the focus of Eastern, Greek-speaking Christianity. In 451, a church council decreed that Constantinople was second only to Rome in ecclesiastical importance. By 500, Constantinople was the richest city in the world.

SUMMARY

_____ was the focal city in the Adolescent Church Era.

- *Hippo* (9). Hippo, a seaport west of Carthage, was a center of early Christianity. Between 391 and 430, it was the home of the famed theologian, Augustine.

Self-Test

Check previous pages for the answers.

A. Match the important places of the Infant Church Era with their descriptions.

Mediterranean Sea   Judea   Italy
Rome

_____ The Ancient Church developed around this body of water.

_____ Focal city of the Infant Church Era.

_____ The cradle of Christianity.

_____ Birthplace of the Roman Empire.

B. Fill in the important places for the Adolescent Church Era.

Ireland and Scotland   Constantinople   Hippo
Celtic Church

_____ _____ _____ were evangelized during
the Adolescent Church Era.

_____ was the focal city in the Adolescent
Church Era.

_____ Taught Scripture and emphasized
evangelism

_____ City associated with the theologian
Augustine.

FIVE

STORY LINE: INFANT CHURCH ERA

Frank Elia has an unusual job. He works in an eight-sided, two-level, glass building. His office contains no books, papers, or metal furniture. It is filled with trees, shrubs, and—butterflies!

Since 1988, lepidopterist Frank Elia has managed the Day Butterfly Center at Callaway Gardens in Pine Mountain, Georgia. It is the largest, free-flight butterfly conservatory in North America.

"There are other butterfly centers," says Mr. Elia, "but the Day Butterfly Center is unique in structure, size, and complexity. If I could describe it in one word, I'd say there's *grandeur* here."

Indeed, there is. The sunny garden is filled with sheltering trees, brick pathways, lush greenery, gay flowers, a waterfall, and high humidity. It is an eight thousand square foot reproduction of an Amazon River environment, a high-tech backdrop for butterflies.

On sunny days, moving insects are all you notice. The air pulsates with flutter, as nearly one thousand tropical butterflies choreograph their short, two-week lifespan. They dart and swerve and glide, a dazzling parade of pigment and pattern. Only gradually do other aspects of this special world come into focus—feeding stations, incubators, caterpillars, birds, and ducks.

Birds and ducks? Most people are surprised to learn that the center is home to other creatures. Hummingbirds dash from flower to flower. Mandarin ducks peer shyly from a pool's edge. Crested wood partridges scurry to find cover, and bleeding heart doves, with their red-splotched breasts, arouse curiosity. The birds serve a purpose; they eat dead butterflies as well as butterfly predators.

Slowly, a visitor becomes a part of the butterfly's world, and the longer one lingers, the more one understands.[1]

A trip through the Infant Church Era is much like a visit to the butterfly center. It is a special environment, pulsating with activity, and the longer one lingers, the more one understands.

As we begin to explore the Infant Church Era, we will follow a pattern that will be used in other Story Line chapters:

1. We will review the era, the date, the epoch, and the pivotal church figure, which we learned in previous chapters.

2. We will read a brief summary of the events of the era, built around the pivotal church figure. Three words will appear in italics. You will be asked to insert these three words on the blanks in a summary box.

3. You will read an expansion of the summary of the events of that era.

4. A self-test will conclude the chapter.

The Infant Church Era

I. Review:

Fill in the blanks for the story of Church History.

Period	Era	Date	Epoch	Pivotal Church Figure	Story Line
	Infant		Pentecost Sunday		
		325–600		Theologians	
Medieval Church	Roman		Gregory the Great		
		1300–1550		Reformers	
Modern Church	Denominational		Council of Trent		
		1789–Present		Strategists	

II. Story Line Summary:

Bishops *guided* the churches as the congregations grew, developed distinct *life-styles,* and suffered *persecution.*

SUMMARY

Bishops _____ the churches as the congregations grew, developed distinct _____ , and suffered_____ .

III. Expansion:

Four distinguishing characteristics of the Infant Church Era were:

1. Growth

2. Life-style

3. Leadership

4. Persecution

1. Growth: Christianity spread rapidly. Early on Pentecost morning in Jerusalem, around A.D. 30, there were about one hundred twenty followers of Jesus Christ. None of them lived in Rome. Yet, by A.D. 300, Rome sheltered a Christian community of over one hundred thousand, and in the Eastern Empire, particularly Greece and Asia Minor, 25 percent of the population was Christian.

The astounding growth of the Infant Church was due to: (1) a common, unifying language, (2) an empire-wide dispersion of the Jews, who opened their synagogues to the Christians, and (3) the *Pax Romana*—two centuries of order, peace, and unprecedented opportunities for travel. Tertullian (c. 150–c. 212), the Christian sage, spoke of the growth: "We are but of yesterday, and we have filled every place among you—cities, islands, fortresses, towns, marketplaces, palace, senate, forum—we have left nothing to you but the temples of your gods."[2]

2. Life-style: Ethics set Christians apart. Christians were known for their ethical life-styles. Because they were neither pagans nor Jews, they were dubbed "the third race."

One observer noted:

They marry and have children just like everyone else; but they do not kill unwanted babies. They offer a shared table, but not a shared bed. They are at present "in the flesh" but they do not live "according to the flesh." . . . They obey appointed laws and go beyond the laws in their own lives.[3]

Christians refused to serve in the Roman army (although service bestowed citizenship), yet they prayed faithfully for the emperor and the empire. Most of all, Christians evangelized. They told citizens and slaves about Jesus, the risen Christ, who offered pardon from sin, peace with God, eternal life, and hope in a hopeless world.

3. Leadership: Dedicated Fathers shepherded the Church. The phrase, *the Fathers of the Church,* referred to four overlapping categories of specialized leadership:

- apostolic fathers
- apologists

- polemicists
- theologians

Apostolic fathers were men who had been taught by the apostles and who, in turn, taught in the church. *Apologists* defended Christianity from pagan criticism and sought legal recognition for the faith. *Polemicists* wrote against the false teachings (heresies) which arose within the church. *Theologians* attempted to harmonize truth with contemporary thinking; they developed methods for study and biblical interpretation. (Although theologians functioned during the Infant Church Era, the notable theologians of the Ancient Period belong to the Adolescent Church Era.) Many of the church fathers were bishops; others were teachers and writers.

4. Persecution: Attacks were scattered and intermittent. Christians were misfits in the Roman world, and, as such, were persecuted periodically. Tertullian wrote:

> If the Tiber floods the city, or if the Nile refuses to rise, or if the sky withholds its rain, if there is an earthquake, a famine, a pestilence, at once the cry is raised: "Christians to the lions."[4]

Persecution was not constant, and it was usually local, prompted by quarrelsome individuals or angry mobs. Government officials, whose chief goal was peacekeeping, used a variety of repressive measures—harassment, torture, fines, banishment, or martyrdom—to maintain order. Several emperors (see list below) subscribed to a "policy of persecution," but only Decius and Diocletian launched all-out campaigns to eradicate the faith. Church leaders were frequently the targets of persecution.

Prominent Emperors Who Persecuted Christians During the Infant Church Era	
Date	**Emperor**
54–68	Nero
82–96	Domitian

Date	Emperor
98–117	Trajan
117–138	Hadrian
139–161	Antoninus Pius
161–180	Marcus Aurelius
193–211	Septimus Severus
249–251	Decius
303–305	Diocletian

Self-Test

To check your answers, review the previous pages.

A. The four characteristics of the Infant Church Era. (Write the characteristic next to its descriptive statement.)

Growth   Life-style   Leadership
Persecution

_____ Scattered, intermittent.

_____ Dedicated.

_____ Ethical, evangelistic.

_____ Rapid.

B. Story Line Summary. (Fill in the blanks from memory.)

Bishops _____ the churches as the congregations grew,
developed distinct_____, and suffered_____.

C. Arc of Church History. (Fill in the name of the Eras.)

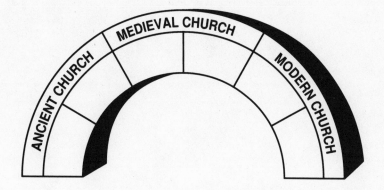

D. Story of Church History. (Fill in the Story of Church History.)

Period	Era	Date	Epoch	Pivotal Church Figure	Story Line
Ancient Church Period					Bishops_____ the churches as the congregations grew, developed distinct _____ and suffered _____.
Medieval Church Period					
Modern Church Period					

SIX

STORY LINE: ADOLESCENT CHURCH ERA

A dolescence prompts a lot of comments:

Adolescents tend to be passionate people, and passion is no less real because it is directed toward a hot-rod, a commercialized popular singer, or the leader of a black-jacketed gang.

Edgar Z. Friedenberg

Adolescence: That period when children feel their parents should be told the facts of life.

Anonymous

The adolescent is a child who is in the process of receiving from the hands of God, through the intermediary of his parents, the personal care of and responsibility for his body, his affection, and his mind.

Michel Quoist

The best thing to do is to behave in a manner befitting one's age. If you are sixteen or under, try not to go bald.

Woody Allen

Remember also your Creator in the days of your youth . . .

Solomon

Adolescence is momentary schizophrenia. It is a time of buoyant misery, selective passion, intolerant tolerance, and constricted enthusiasm.

Adolescence bivouacs in the body, but, as John Keats noted, it camps elsewhere, too. "The imagination of a boy is healthy, and the mature imagination of a man is healthy; but there is a space of life between, in which the soul is in ferment, the character undecided, the way of life uncertain."[1]

The dictionary defines *adolescence*—this "space of life" —as a stage of development that precedes maturity.

The church in A.D. 325 was a normal adolescent. Protected by the state, it strutted a new style, trading its childlike cloak of faith for the vestments of bureaucratic aristocracy. Reality restructured its outlook. Acceptance jogged its character. Controversy blared from its soul. For nearly three hundred years, A.D. 325–600, the church struggled to establish its identity, to clarify its values, and to codify its beliefs.

Let's examine some of the colorful personalities and trying circumstances that shaped the Adolescent Church Era.

The Adolescent Church Era

I. Review:

Fill in the blanks for the Story of Church History.

Period	Era	Date	Epoch	Pivotal Church Figure	Story Line
					Bishops _____ the churches as the congregations grew, developed distinct _____ , and suffered_____ .

II. Story Line Summary:

Theologians *organized* the church, upheld its *authority*, and continued its *traditions*.

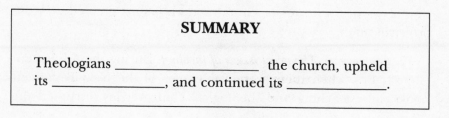

SUMMARY

Theologians _____ the church, upheld its _____, and continued its _____.

III. Expansion:

Four factors that influenced the Adolescent Church Era were:

1. Constantine

2. Controversy

3. Institutionalization

4. Invasion

1. Constantine: The first Christian emperor. Constantine was the pagan emperor whose conversion changed Christianity. Constantine accepted Christ in 312 before the battle of Milvian Bridge. According to the emperor, he prayed to the "Supreme God" for help, and in response, a cross appeared in the midday sky along with the message: "Conquer by this." That night Christ appeared to Constantine and ordered him to use the Chi-Rho "as a safeguard in all engagements with his enemies."[2]

While critics debate the veracity of the event, few can deny that the conversion of Constantine turned the world upside down. Constantine gave Christianity status. He safeguarded the church, built official church buildings, and exempted the clergy from taxes. He encouraged worship and instituted a day of rest, which he called Sun-day, after a pagan god.

Constantine upheld the belief that the state was the "bearer" of religion and the emperor was God's representative on earth. Constantine interjected himself in the workings of the church, setting policies and establishing practices. Not all the clergy appreciated him. Some, like Donatus, a North African bishop, asked: "What has the emperor to do with the Church?"[3] Others hailed Constantine as the power who could evangelize the world. From Constantine forward, the issues of church-state relations gnawed at Western civilization.

2. Controversy: The great issues of theology. During the Adolescent Church Era, when there were few copies of the New Testament books, false teaching and theological controversies disrupted the church. To restore harmony, theologians formulated creeds—summary statements of faith which were memorized by believers.

The great issues of theology involved the Trinity, the deity of Christ, the Person of the Holy Spirit, and the nature and salvation of man. The disputes regarding the Trinity, Christ, and the Holy Spirit bubbled up in the Eastern (Greek) church. The controversy over man and his salvation originated in the Western (Latin) church.

3. Institutionalization: The formation of policy. Under Constantine, church life grew more complex. Practices became policies. Doctrines became dogmas—statements of official position. Worship became ceremony. Church councils were created, and ecclesiastical lines of authority were drawn. Partiality was shown to the bishops at Rome, Constantinople, Antioch, Alexandria, and Jerusalem. A "corporate ladder" was established—ambitious clerics could be readers, the lowest official position in the church, at age ten and bishops by forty-five.

4. Invasion: The barbarians attack the empire. During the Infant Church Era, Rome protected its population (fifty to sixty million people) and its nearly ten thousand miles of border with an army of 450,000. Along its northern frontiers nestled restless Germanic tribes—Angles, Saxons, Goths, Vandals, and Franks—all commonly referred to as "the barbarians." The barbarians were an uncivilized lot, but they longed to be a part of the empire. At first they came as immigrants under a policy instituted by Augustus (63 B.C.–A.D. 14). Early barbarians settled frontier areas, joined the Roman army, and engaged in commerce. As the empire weakened, the barbarians became invaders.

During the fourth and fifth centuries, the irruption of the Huns in Central Asia triggered a turbulent wave of barbarian migration in China, India, Persia, and Europe. The Roman Empire was hard hit. In 410, Alaric the Goth sacked Rome. Hordes descended on Gaul. The Angles and Saxons overran Britain. The Vandals attacked North Africa. Attila and his 500,000 marauders terrorized the Eastern Empire for a decade and finally invaded Italy in 452. In 476, Rome "fell" when a barbarian officer in the

Roman army deposed the last Roman emperor and, in effect, established himself as king of Italy.

While the church was busily settling controversies and deciding policies, the society into which it had been born disintegrated, and Western civilization did not recover for 700 years.

Self-Test

A. Four factors that influenced the Adolescent Church Era. (Match the factors with their descriptive statements below.)

Constantine   Controversy   Invasion
Institutionalization

_____ The barbarians attack the empire.

_____ Establishing official church policy and practices.

_____ The first Christian emperor.

_____ Debates over the great issues of theology.

B. Story Line Summary. (Fill in the blanks from memory.)

Theologians_____ the church, upheld its _____, and continued its _____.

C. Arc of Church History. (Fill in the Arc of Church History.)

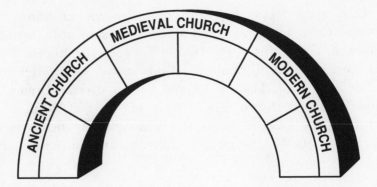

D. Story of Church History. (Fill in the Story of Church History.)

Period	Era	Date	Epoch	Pivotal Church Figure	Story Line
					Bishops _____ the churches as the congregations grew, developed distinct _____, and suffered _____.
					Theologians _____ the church, upheld its _____, and continued its _____.

SEVEN

HEADLINES:
ANCIENT
CHURCH PERIOD

A ccording to the *Chicago Tribune,* a newspaper is "an institution developed by modern civilization to present the news of the day . . . , to lead and inform public opinion, and to furnish that check upon government which no constitution has ever been able to provide."[1]

Julius Caesar may have inspired the definition.

In 58 B.C., Caesar's relations with the Roman Senate were strained. To arouse public support, Caesar paid clerks to record the Senate's proceedings on the walls of the forums—the marketplaces in the business district. The messages, called *Acta Diurna* ("Daily Doings"), were copied and sent to all parts of the empire along with records of births, deaths, divorces, edicts, executions, marriages, and other news. Thus, in theory, the newspaper was born.

News crackled during the Ancient Church Period. There was scandal. There was weather. There were wars and rumors of wars. Sports, fashion, and entertainment vied for attention.

While it would be impossible to capture all the headlines, we will sample four front-page features from the Ancient Church Period under the headings: NEWS, MONEY, SPORTS, and LIFE. Each feature adds to our understanding and helps to paint a picture of the society that buffeted Christianity.

NEWS

DISASTER PLAGUES EMPIRE

Dateline: Pompeii; 24 August A.D. 79. Mt. Vesuvius convulsed and belched rock and fire on the sleepy resort town of Pompeii, fifteen miles southeast of Naples. The initial explosion occurred around noon and jolted townsfolk who were enjoying a late summer holiday. Festivities were halted as heavy rain turned volcanic debris into a fast-moving wall of mud and ash that buried the city to its rooftops within six hours.

Tidal waves and poor visibility hampered escape. Clouds filled with pumice and poisonous gas blackened the skies. Refugees tied pillows to their heads, hoping to protect themselves from the downpour of rock. Many who sought shelter in buildings were asphyxiated by gas or buried under rubble.

The noted scientist and scholar, Pliny the Elder, is listed among the two thousand dead. Pliny, an imperial naval commander stationed in the Bay of Naples, had sailed to Pompeii to give aid and satisfy his famed curiosity. His body was discovered on the beaches outside the city.

The disaster at Pompeii followed closely the devastating spring fires in Rome. Throughout the empire, rumors continue to circulate that the disasters match the "end times" judgment scenario described by the troublesome Christian sect.

Emperor Titus (the general who destroyed Jerusalem in A.D. 70) responded with bountiful generosity to the calamities. It was said that "he showed not merely the concern of an emperor, but a father's surpassing love."[2] ■

MONEY

SPINNING LUCRATIVE THREADS

Dateline: Constantinople; 552. It's hard to pass up a good deal in any age! After centuries of wars with Persia for control of the silk routes to China and India, Emperor Justinian has gained the upper hand.

This year Justinian sent Nestorian monks, a splinter Christian group with unorthodox theology, on a special missionary journey to the Far East. Their assignment was not to win souls but to smuggle out silkworm eggs and mulberry tree saplings, which the monks hid in hollow bamboo canes.

Silk, worth its weight in gold, has been the fabric of choice for aristocrats since A.D. 96. The monks' spoils have launched the empire toward a profitable business monopoly. Justinian is cultivating both silk and dye production in Constantinople and reserving the finest fabrics for imperial and Church use. ■

SPORTS

TIME-OUT, ROMAN STYLE

Dateline: Rome; A.D. 107. After four months of frenetic celebration, Rome uttered a final thanks for its conquest of Dacia (modern Romania), raised a last toast to its military genius, Emperor Trajan, and slumped into a euphoric stupor. For 123 days, victory intoxicated the city, and Rome, which warred hard, played hard.

Rome's chief diversions were the public games—theater, circus, and combats. Theater titillated crowds with staged horseplay, coarse slapstick, vulgar character studies, licentious pantomime, and sensual dance. The quest for realism pushed dramatists to the razor's edge. When a drama included a death scene, the actor was replaced by a prisoner who was poisoned, stabbed, or strangled, while the audience hissed, cheered, or booed.

The circus fueled Rome's mania for gambling. Chariot drivers from professional "schools" and local prisoners seeking to win their freedom breached whimsical rules to win the "Ave!" of the crowd. Spectators bet heavily, and fortunes were made or lost in seven laps. Frenzy reigned; riots broke out. Life expectancies for drivers and horses were short and only slightly better for the unruly spectators. Winning drivers were well-paid and lavishly adulated; the streets of Rome reverberated with the names of heroes.

For sheer popularity and brutality, however, nothing during the celebration matched the combats. Each morning, crowds jammed the Colosseum as wild beasts took center stage. Animal fought animal—a tigress against a bull elephant, a leopard against a bear. Then, animals fought humans, and thousands of Jews, Christians, and slaves died while crowds chanted, "Kill! Kill!"

After lunch and a brief intermission, gladiators fought wild animals or other gladiators. Man-against-man combats often matched men of unequal skills and strengths. Contests were "to the death," but crowds occasionally spared the life of a fallen gladiator. Although arena attendants used elaborate rope systems to remove the slain or wounded, by mid-afternoon Colosseum floors ran blood red.

During Trajan's nonstop celebration, ten thousand wild and domestic animals were slain and an equal number of gladiators fought. The poet Juvenal once quipped: "The Roman people who once gave commands, consulships, legions, and all else, now yearn simply for two things—free bread and the public games!"[3] For 123 days, Rome was satiated. ∎

![LIFE]

ROME'S HOTTEST SPOT FOR A COOL WORK-OUT

Dateline: Summer; A.D. 217; The Baths of Caracalla. All roads in Rome lead to the Baths of Caracalla as tourists and citizens throng the new, recently opened, state-of-the-art facility.

Nestled in a town already swimming with baths, Emperor Caracalla's latest public works project offers more than a soothing experience in physical luxury. The Baths are an architectural wonder—a complex arrangement of buildings, halls, and courts, covering more than two hundred seventy thousand square feet (larger than England's Houses of Parliament and Westminster Hall combined).[4] The floors and walls are marble, inlaid with intricate mosaic designs. More than two hundred columns and pillars of granite, alabaster, and porphyry lend support and decoration. An abundance of water—hot, tepid, or cool, depending on preference—supplies the pools and basins for sixteen hundred bathers, while other diversions amuse an additional fourteen hundred guests.

For a mere quadran (1½ cents), the Baths of Caracalla offer citizens a sweet sip of unabashed luxury, featuring dressing rooms, steam rooms, massage rooms, athletic fields, pools, a beauty spa, art gallery, and clubhouse.

More goes on at the Baths than bathing. Romans exercise, compete, primp, and watch demonstrations, but they also argue politics, savor gossip, cut business deals, hatch schemes, and make wagers. The more intellectual attend lectures, read books, or listen to poetry. Many customers enjoy the convenience of the dining room, which serves wine with platters of food.

The initial response to the Baths of Caracalla has been overwhelming. The dawn-to-dusk operation has few slow times; many patrons have endured lengthy waits to enjoy the facilities. The Baths have quickly become one of the trendiest locations in the empire and certainly deserve a five-sponge rating. ∎

Self-Test

A. Complete the Arc of Church History.

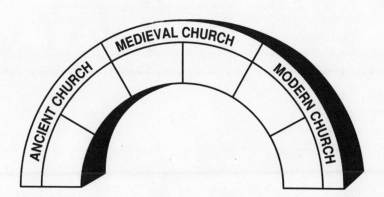

B. Complete the Story of Church History.

Period	Era	Date	Epoch	Pivotal Church Figure	Story Line
					Bishops _____ the churches as the congregations grew, developed distinct _____, and suffered _____.
					Theologians _____ the church, upheld its _____ , and continued its _____.

EIGHT

CONCEPTS: ANCIENT CHURCH PERIOD

O ne day, Mrs. Noah Webster happened into the parlor, where she discovered her husband embracing the maid. "Noah, I am surprised!" she gasped. Webster, the author of America's famed dictionary, stepped back, regained his composure, and corrected, "No, my dear, it is *I* who am surprised; you are merely astonished."[1]

Although the authenticity of this story is somewhat doubtful, Mr. Webster well understood the precision of language. With over seven hundred ninety thousand entries, English is the wordiest language in the world. Therefore, it is not surprising that a subject like church history might contain some confusing words. The Ancient Church, for instance, had problems with the pagans—or was it the heathens? What's a pagan? What's a heathen? What's the difference?

The Ancient Church had trouble with both pagans and heathen. The term *pagan* referred to the rural classes, the peasants of the Roman Empire. The Infant Church was urban in outreach and made no attempt to convert the pagans, but, over the years, *pagan* came to mean pre-Christian people who worshiped many gods.

The barbarians were called *heathen*. The heathen did not worship the God of the Bible, and their behavior was deemed uncivilized because they ignored the so-called genteel customs of the Greeks and Romans. Today we use the terms *heathen* and *pagan* to mean non-Christian.

Because concepts help us understand the eras, we will begin our study of the Ancient Church Period by looking at four concepts that dominated the Infant Church Era and four that dominated the Adolescent Church Era. The outstanding concept of each era will be examined first. At the end of the outstanding concept section, a summary box will appear for you to complete. You will then be introduced to three other important concepts. At the end of each era, a self-test will help you evaluate what you have learned.

The outstanding concept is particularly important because it will begin a wheel chart which will be used throughout the era. The five components of the chart are reproduced below.

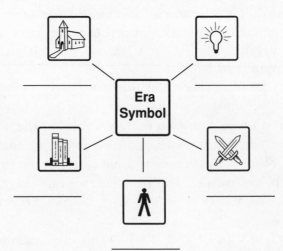

At the center of the wheel chart is the special symbol for the church era. Beginning with the upper right-hand corner and moving clockwise, the spokes on the wheel represent the five major areas of our study: concepts, foes, key figures, writers/writings, and trends.

This chapter and the following four chapters will successively address each of these five major areas as they relate to the two eras of the Ancient Church Period.

The Infant Church Era

I. The Outstanding Concept: Orthodoxy

During the Infant Church Era, bishops began to codify the orthodox beliefs of Christianity. The word *orthodoxy* came from two Greek words, *orthos* meaning "right" or "straight," and *doxa* meaning "praise" or "glory." Beliefs that were orthodox agreed with established truths (the basic body of Christian practices and teachings as derived from Scripture), apostolic doctrine (elementary principles of the faith), tradition (the way the first-century church understood the teachings of Jesus), liturgical practices, and authoritative writings. Today, the term *orthodoxy* is used interchangeably with the phrase "historical biblical Christianity."

SUMMARY

The outstanding concept of the Infant Church Era was _____.

II. Summary of Other Important Concepts:

1. Heresy

2. Gnosticism

3. Asceticism

1. Heresy: Serious doctrinal error. Heresy was serious doctrinal error, a teaching that contradicted Scripture, and, therefore, was not orthodox. Heretics denied or altered fundamental Christian beliefs, such as the divinity of Christ, and disrupted the unity of the church. Heretics were condemned and sometimes ostracized.

A related term was *schism.* Schism was a division in the church for a reason other than doctrine. Schisms, which arose over differences of opinion about patterns of worship or the recognition of authority, were a part of church life by A.D. 185. The "Great Schism" of Christianity occurred in 1054, when the Western (Roman) church separated from the Eastern (Orthodox) church.

2. Gnosticism: The number one heresy of the Infant Church Era. Gnosticism was the most formidable heresy of the Infant Church Era. The word gnosticism came from the Greek word *gnosis,* meaning "knowledge." Gnostics believed that man achieved salvation as he attained a secret knowledge of God through good works, special teaching, and mystical rituals. Gnostics taught that matter was evil and spirit was good. Because Jesus possessed a human nature, the Gnostics denied His deity and atoning work.

Gnosticism was an appealing blend of Christianity, Judaism, Greek philosophy, and Oriental mysticism. Christian leaders, like Justin Martyr and Tertullian, identified Simon Magus (see Acts 8) as the source of gnosticism. Because Gnostics claimed that they represented the only true church, the orthodox church began to call itself the *catholic* (universal) church. "Catholic" bishops, who refuted Gnostic teachings, became the spokesmen for Christianity.

3. Asceticism: The life-style of self-denial. Asceticism was the practice of strict self-denial. The custom was prompted by certain Scripture passages and the life-styles of Jesus and John the Baptist. The practice was further encouraged by an ancient writing, *The Shepherd of Hermas* (c. 140), which urged Christians to a higher, disciplined spirituality.

Ascetics or hermits were laypeople who withdrew to caves, tombs, or the desert to practice holiness in isolation. They prayed, meditated, and read portions of Scripture. (The Bible as we know it had not yet been collected.) Ascetics ate little; some ate grass. A few never bathed. Many slept only a few hours each day.

Asceticism gained popularity between 260 and 303 when there was no persecution and large numbers of pagans embraced Christianity. Pagan commitment was often half-hearted. As a result, church leaders lowered standards. Asceticism was a reaction against the slackening of standards.

Self-Test

A. The important concepts of the Infant Church Era. (Match the concepts with the definitions below.)

Heresy   Orthodoxy   Gnosticism
Asceticism

_____ The most formidable heresy the Infant Church faced.

_____ Agreeing with the basic body of accepted beliefs.

_____ A life-style marked by self-denial.

_____ Serious doctrinal error.

B. The outstanding concept of the Infant Church Era. (Write the outstanding concept on the blank provided.)

The outstanding concept of the Infant Church Era was _____ .

C. Wheel chart. (Place the name of the outstanding concept on the wheel chart.)

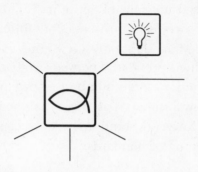

The Adolescent Church Era

I. The outstanding concept: Church councils

Church councils were ecumenical (worldwide) meetings of invited representatives, usually bishops, from the known world. When Constantine convened the first church council, the Council of Nicea, in 325, he borrowed the conciliar pattern used by the Infant Church in A.D. 49. (See Acts 15.) Church councils produced the great statements of faith and enacted mandates which were binding on the entire church.

The Council of Nicea was especially significant, since it was the first meeting in church history called by an emperor rather than by a church leader. The council produced the Nicene Creed, but it also encouraged ecclesiastical rivalry by elevating the bishops of certain cities to places of importance.

The first seven councils, which met between 325 and 787, were the only councils recognized by the Eastern Orthodox church and by many of the Protestant churches. Today, the Roman Catholic church recognizes twenty-one ecumenical councils; the most recent was Vatican II in 1962.

The church councils prompted two far-reaching activities, *anathematize* and *excommunicate*, which related to punishment. To anathematize meant to banish completely. To excommunicate meant to exclude a guilty party from worship and the sacraments. Excommunication, though serious, was the milder form of punishment.

SUMMARY

The outstanding concept of the Adolescent Church Era
was _____ _____ .

II. Summary of other important concepts:

1. Creeds

2. Eastern church/Western church

3. Monasticism

1. Creeds: Statements of faith. Creeds were simple statements of New Testament faith. Some were short and informal. Others, like the Nicene Creed, were more complex. Creeds were an important part of the oral tradition of the early church because they summarized major teachings, formed a unified body of beliefs, and were easy to memorize.

Unlike the Nicene Creed, the Apostles' Creed was not developed by a council. The Apostles' Creed was a baptismal statement that converts memorized. It was originally called "the Old Roman Creed" and early texts date it to around 400. The Apostle's Creed became the standard baptismal confession of the West, while the Nicene Creed was used in the East.

2. Eastern church/Western church: One church with two traditions. The bishops who came to the ecumenical councils were from two different traditions: the Eastern church—represented by Greece, Asia Minor, Syria, and Egypt, and the Western church—represented by Rome, North Africa, and Gaul. Although the word *catholic* (universal) was used to describe the whole body of Christianity, Christians and their bishops referenced their faith by their distinct cultures. Consequently, conflicts arose.

The Eastern church spoke Greek, and the Western church spoke Latin. The two traditions spent fifty years haggling over one important word in a creed. They disagreed about the use of icons (images), Lenten practices, the date for celebrating Easter, the bread used in the Eucharist, the style of hymns, and the marital status of clergy. When Emperor Theodosius divided the empire between his two sons in 395, the cultural alignment was set.

3. Monasticism: Communal asceticism. Monasticism, which originated in the Eastern church, added a new twist to asceticism. Monks were still secluded from the world, but they lived in communities rather than in isolation. Antony of Egypt (c. 256–356) was called "the father of monasticism," but his countryman, Pachomius, founded the first monastery (c. 320).

Basil the Great (c. 330–379) gave monasticism its structure. Basil founded a monastery (c. 358) in Asia Minor and tied it to a local church. Under the authority of the bishop, Basil's monastery cared for the poor, nursed the sick, established a school, and looked after lepers. Basil introduced the concept of the seven prayer periods into the monastic day.

Monasticism moved to the West around 375, where men like Jerome and Augustine refined the concept. As the Adolescent Church became entwined in secular affairs and as church offices became more susceptible to political influences, the monasteries became a haven for Christians who wanted a purer environment for their faith.

Self-Test

A. The important concepts of the Adolescent Church Era. (Match the concepts with the definitions below.)

Creeds   Church councils   Monasticism
Eastern church/Western church

_____ An ecumenical or worldwide meeting of bishops.

_____ A communal life-style marked by work and prayer.

_____ The cultural traditions that dominated the church.

_____ Statements of faith.

B. The outstanding concepts of the Adolescent Church Era. (Write the great concept on the blank provided.)

The outstanding concept of the Adolescent Church Era was

_____   _____.

C. Wheel chart. (Place the name of the outstanding concept on the wheel chart.)

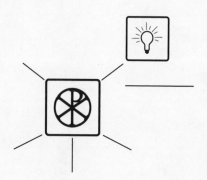

NINE

FOES: ANCIENT CHURCH PERIOD

C astruccio Castracani, the leader of a band of medieval Italian mercenaries, was a longtime friend of the Quatigiani family of Lucca. After many years, they quarreled and fought. Castracani defeated them and afterward dealt harshly with them. Chided by an aide for dealing so severely with old friends, Castracani replied, "I am not dealing with old friends but with new enemies."[1]

The Ancient Church had no shortage of enemies. During the Infant Church Era, its foes came primarily from *outside* the Church. During the Adolescent Church Era, the foes came from *inside* the Church. The names of the outside foes are familiar to us—the names of the Roman emperors. The inside foes are not nearly as well known. They were clergymen who taught error and challenged the authority of the church.

In the material that follows we will examine the effects that four emperors and four teachers had on the Ancient Church. The name of the major foe from each era is enclosed in a boxed statement.

The Infant Church Era

I. Review:

Fill in the wheel chart to bring the era up to date.

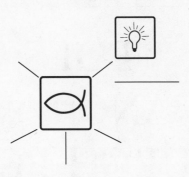

II. The major foe: Diocletian

Diocletian (284–305), emperor during the closing days of the Infant Church Era, was a soldier and a master statesman who ruled for twenty-one years—longer than any emperor in the previous century and a half. Diocletian left Rome and moved his headquarters to Nicomedia (near Constantinople) to be close to the trouble spots. There, he skillfully thwarted the barbarians, offset economic decline, and reorganized the empire under a tetrarchy, a four-man rulership.

But, Diocletian could not manage the church, which was wealthy, growing, well-organized, and in an age of apathy, contained people with strong beliefs. (Diocletian's wife Prisca and daughter Valeria were Christians.)

Urged by his son Galerius, Diocletian tried to eradicate Christianity. Beginning in Nicomedia, soldiers burnt Scriptures, destroyed buildings, scattered congregations, and confiscated property. Believers throughout the empire were persecuted, jailed, or executed. Many were disfigured: ears were cut off; flesh was seared; noses were slit or bones brutally dislocated. Bishop Paphnutius of

Egypt, later a delegate to the Council of Nicea, had his right eye gouged out and his left knee crushed. Only Gaul and Britain escaped the brutality known as the Great Persecution.

Diocletian retired in 305, but the oppression continued under his son. Not until 311 did the dying Galerius issue an edict of toleration and ask for the prayers of the Christians.

SUMMARY

_____ was the major foe of the Infant Church Era.

III. Summary of other foes:

1. Nero

2. Trajan

3. Decius

1. Nero: The emperor who labeled Christians "criminals." History paints a doleful picture of Nero (54–68). He murdered. He schemed. His passions controlled him. His interaction with the Infant Church was grim. He was the first emperor to label Christians "criminals."

On July 18 A.D. 64, fire broke out in Rome and raged for nine days. Ten of the fourteen quarters of the city were destroyed. Thousands were homeless. Nero was blamed. He looked for a scapegoat, and Tacitus tells us he settled on

> a race of men detested for their evil practices, and commonly called *Chrestiani* [Christians]. The name was derived from Chrestus, who, in the reign of Tiberius, suffered under Pontius Pilate, Procurator of Judea. . . . He [Nero] found a set of profligate and abandoned wretches who were induced to confess themselves guilty; and on the evidence of such men a number of Christians were convicted, not indeed on clear evidence of having set the city on fire, but rather on account of their sullen hatred of the whole human race. They were put to death with

exquisite cruelty, and to their sufferings Nero added mockery
and derision. Some were covered with skins of wild beasts, and
left to be devoured by dogs; others were nailed to crosses; numbers of them were burned alive; many, covered with inflammable
matter, were set on fire to serve as torches during the night. . . .
At length the brutality of these measures filled every breast with
pity. Humanity relented in favor of the Christians.[2]

Somewhere among the "scapegoats" were Peter and Paul,
along with Aristarchus and Trophimus, two companions from
Paul's third missionary journey (Acts 19:29; 20:4).[3]

**2. Trajan: The emperor who set policy against the Chris-
tians.** Trajan (98–117), one of the five "good" Roman emperors,
was an accomplished soldier, an excellent administrator, and an
unselfish ruler. Under his leadership, the empire blossomed. Trajan was so respected that 250 years after his death, the Senate bestowed blessings on a new emperor by wishing that he might
"surpass the felicity of Augustus and the virtue of Trajan."[4]

Trajan is known in church history as the emperor who first set
imperial policy against the Christians. In 112, Trajan received a
letter from Pliny the Younger, the governor of Bithynia in Asia
Minor, asking for help. Pliny wanted to know whether he should
punish Christians according to the law even when they had committed no offense other than being "Christian." Trajan replied:

Do like this. They [Christians] are not to be hunted out. [Al-
though] any who are accused and convicted should be punished,
with the proviso that if a man says he is not a Christian and
makes it obvious by his actual conduct—namely, by worshipping
our gods—then, however suspect he may have been with regard
to the past, he should gain pardon from his repentance.[5]

Under Trajan's policy, the revered Ignatius, bishop of Antioch,
was fed to the lions, probably in the famous Colosseum at Rome.

**3. Decius: The first emperor to launch a widescale attack on
Christianity.** Chaos ruled the third century. The barbarians invaded. The provinces revolted. The economy was strained, and emperors were murdered regularly. (In the year 238, there were six

emperors.) Into this atmosphere marched Emperor Decius (249–251), a soldier with a plan.

In 248, Rome celebrated its 1000th anniversary, an event that produced a veneer of nationalism. Believing that a mass demonstration of religious fervor would unite the empire, Decius ordered all subjects to publicly sacrifice to the Roman gods and thereby receive a special certificate (*libelli*) proving their loyalty. The decree, a public affront to Christianity, became the first empire-wide attack on Christianity.

According to Cyprian, the bishop of Carthage, multitudes of Christians sacrificed or quietly bought certificates from sympathetic officials.[6] Many Christians, however, scorned the Roman gods, openly predicted the destruction of the empire, and were persecuted. Hundreds, including well-known church leaders, were jailed or martyred. Fabian, the bishop of Rome, and Babylas of Antioch were beheaded. Origen in Caesarea was tortured, suffering "under an iron collar, . . . when for many days he was extended and stretched to the distance of four holes on the rack; besides the threats of fire, and whatsoever other sufferings inflicted by his enemies."[7] Decius died in 251, but the persecutions continued through 260.

Self-Test

A. The foes of the Infant Church Era. (Identify the Roman emperors who opposed the Infant Church.)

Trajan   Decius   Nero
Diocletian

_____ Launched the first empire-wide persecution.

_____ First set imperial policy against Christians.

_____ Ordered the Great Persecution.

_____ Accused the Christians of burning Rome.

B. The major foe of the Infant Church Era. (Write the major foe on the blank provided.)

_____ was the major foe of the Infant Church Era.

C. Wheel chart. (Place the name of the major foe on the wheel chart.)

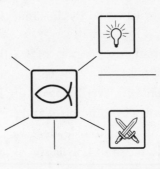

The Adolescent Church Era

I. Review:

Fill in the wheel chart to bring the era up to date.

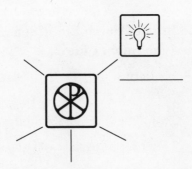

II. The major foe: Arius

Arius was a popular teacher in Alexandria, Egypt. In 318, he denied the deity of Christ by claiming that the Father alone was God and that Jesus, His created Son, was different and not of the same substance. "The Son has a beginning," Arius wrote, "but . . . God is without beginning."[8] A synod, a regional meeting of bishops, denounced his ideas, but the controversy escalated.

In 325, the Council of Nicea officially condemned Arius and formulated the Nicene Creed to offset his doctrinal error. The Nicene Creed stated the orthodox position: "We believe in one God, . . . And in one Lord Jesus Christ, . . . begotten, not made, being of one substance with the Father."[9]

Arius himself was banished to Illyrium (modern Yugoslavia), where his teaching was widely accepted, especially by the invading barbarians, who later carried it into Western Europe.

Arianism was an extremely popular, highly divisive teaching that disrupted the church until leaders settled the issue in 381. Today, Arius is honored by the Jehovah's Witnesses.

SUMMARY

_____ was the major foe of the Adolescent Church Era.

III. Summary of other foes:

1. Donatus

2. Nestorius

3. Pelagius

1. Donatus: The schismatic bishop. Donatus was a bishop in Carthage (313–355) who led some of the North African churches into schism by challenging the authority of the church. Donatus and his followers, the Donatists, believed that anyone who had handed over the Scriptures to be burned during the Great Persecution was an apostate, one who had abandoned the faith, and was never to be forgiven.

The Donatists objected to the selection of an "apostate" as an orthodox bishop. A dispute arose, and a local ruling body favored the orthodox bishop. The Donatists appealed to Constantine. When the emperor upheld the decision, the Donatists balked and violence erupted.

A radical Donatist organization, the Circumcellions, emerged and tied the controversial religious issues to nationalistic struggles. The Donatist church claimed that it was the only true church and joined an unsuccessful revolt against Rome. Gradually, North Africa became a region with two distinct churches, the orthodox church and the militant Donatist church.

The Donatists were active in Hippo when Augustine became bishop, and he opposed them. Augustine's disgust was obvious: "The clouds roll with thunder, that the house of the Lord shall be built throughout the earth; and these frogs sit in their marsh and croak 'We are the only Christians'!"[10]

2. Nestorius: The heretical bishop. Nestorius was the patriarch (lead bishop) of Constantinople who, in 428, sparked another heresy. Nestorius taught that the divine nature and the human nature of Christ were not united. "I hold the natures apart but unite the worship," he said.[11]

To settle the issue, the emperor convened the Council of Ephesus in 431, which condemned the teaching of Nestorius. Because many points of protocol were breached in the conduct of the conciliar meeting, Nestorius's position in Church history has remained clouded.

After 431, Nestorianism did not die, but adherents of the movement moved to Edessa and propagated the belief. Nestorians made converts in Arabia, southwestern India, Turkestan (the area east of the Caspian Sea), Tibet, and central China. In 486, Nestorianism became the official teaching of the Persian church. Today,

Nestorians number eighty thousand in Iraq, Iran, and Syria, with an additional twenty-five thousand members in the United States.

3. Pelagius: The heretical monk. Pelagius was an ascetic British monk who opposed major orthodox teachings in the Church. Pelagius denied original sin, maintained that some men lived sinless lives, negated the power of the Holy Spirit in a regenerate life, and taught that salvation was not an act of grace.

Two giants of the church, Augustine in Hippo and Jerome in Jerusalem, began battling Pelagianism around 412. Augustine reiterated the biblical position on sin and developed his doctrine of grace, while Jerome wrote his *Dialogues against the Pelagians* in 415. Pelagianism entered the church through Rome and quickly spread through the North African churches and into Palestine as Pelagian refugees fled the barbarian attack on Rome in 411. Both Jerome and Augustine died before the church officially condemned the heresy at the controversial Council of Ephesus in 431.

Self-Test

A. The foes of the Adolescent Church Era. (Identify the teachers who challenged the Adolescent Church.)

Arius   Nestorius   Pelagius
Donatus

_____ Divided the natures of Christ.

_____ Denied the deity of Christ.

_____ Led North Africans into schism.

_____ Rejected the concept of original sin.

B. The major foe of the Adolescent Church Era. (Write the foe on the blank provided.)

_____ was the major foe of the Adolescent Church Era.

C. Wheel chart. (Place the name of the major foe on the wheel chart.)

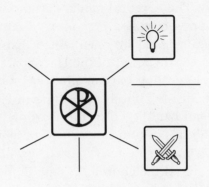

TEN

KEY FIGURES: ANCIENT CHURCH PERIOD

T he Perseids. They are not a rock group, a financial index, or the latest computer software. They are meteors that inscribe paths across the night sky during August. The Perseids contain two types of objects: faint meteors called "shooting stars," which usually cannot be seen, and bright meteors called "fireballs" that light up the sky.

Like the Perseids, thousands of "shooting stars" have flashed across the canopy of church history. We, however, have time to gaze only at "fireballs"—eight luminaries with dazzling credentials. Four of these important men are associated with the Infant Church Era and four belong to the Adolescent Church Era. The key figure from each era will appear in a boxed statement.

The Infant Church Era

I. Review:

Fill in the blanks to bring the wheel chart up to date.

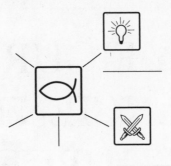

II. Key figure: Ignatius

Ignatius (c. 70–c. 110), the third bishop of Antioch, opposed false teachers and helped organize the church into a three-tiered organizational structure that included a single bishop (monepiscopacy), elders, and deacons. He was the first person to use the term *Christianity* and to call the church *catholic,* meaning universal. "Wherever Jesus Christ is," wrote Ignatius, "there is the catholic church."[1]

Under Emperor Trajan (98–117), Ignatius was arrested and escorted to Rome by ten surly soldiers. En route, he wrote seven letters of encouragement—six to churches and one to Polycarp, bishop of Smyrna. The letters reveal the concerns of a dedicated bishop and include a plea not to interfere with his martyrdom:

> I . . . am insisting to everyone that I die for God of my own free will—unless you hinder me. I implore you: do not be unseasonably kind to me. . . . Suffer me to be eaten by the beasts, through whom I can attain to God. I am God's wheat, and I am ground by the teeth of wild beasts that I may be found pure bread of Christ.[2]

Ignatius was fed to the lions about A.D. 110.

SUMMARY

_____ was the key figure of the Infant Church Era.

III. Summary of other important figures:

1. Polycarp

2. Justin Martyr

3. Irenaeus

1. Polycarp: Bishop and martyr. Polycarp (c. 70–156), the bishop of Smyrna for fifty years, was a mid-second-century policymaker who opposed false teachers and helped settle the canon of the New Testament. His writing, "The Letter of Polycarp to the Philippians" (c. 110), revealed his deep pastoral concerns and his great familiarity with the New Testament documents. He also supported monepiscopal church organization and urged faithfulness in the face of persecution.

Like Ignatius, Polycarp was martyred. His execution was recorded by eyewitnesses. When Polycarp was asked to revile Christ in exchange for his life, he replied: "Eighty and six years have I served him, and he hath done me no wrong; how then can I blaspheme my King who saved me?"[3] Outside of the New Testament, the account of Polycarp's death is the oldest record of a martyrdom.

2. Justin Martyr: The leading apologist of the early Church. Justin Martyr (c. 100–165) was a Gentile, well-schooled in philosophy. A conversation with an old man led him to the Scriptures and to Christ. Afterward, Justin dedicated himself to teaching, writing, and winning converts. He became the most persuasive apologist of the early church, often presenting his views to emperors, pagans, and Jews.

Among Justin's writings were *First Apology,* a "state of the church" message written to Emperor Pius; *Second Apology,* a protest against the martyrdom of some Roman Christians; and *Dialogue with Trypho,* an in-depth look at Jewish-Christian issues. Justin was the first authority to record the traditions that the Magi came from Arabia and that Jesus was born in a cave in Bethlehem.

3. Irenaeus: The polemicist who fought gnosticism. Irenaeus (c. 177–c. 202), the bishop of Lyons, was an outstanding polemicist who fought the heresy called gnosticism. The writings of Irenaeus, particularly *Against Heresies,* helped develop orthodox doctrine. He promoted apostolic succession—the belief that the apostles had faithfully transmitted the teachings of Christ to their successors, the bishops of the orthodox church. Apostolic succession offset the Gnostic claim that the apostles had passed on a secret and exclusive tradition. Irenaeus was the first author whose writings re-flect a canon of the New Testament that was on the same level as the Old Testament.

Self-Test

A. Important figures of the Infant Church Era. (Identify the key figure from the descriptive statements.)

Ignatius   Polycarp   Justin Martyr
Irenaeus

_____ Bishop who promoted monepiscopacy and first used the terms *Christianity* and *catholic.*

_____ Bishop who fought gnosticism.

_____ His death provides the oldest extrabibli-cal account of a martyrdom in Church history.

_____ Defended the faith before emperors, pa-gans, and Jews.

B. Key Figure of the Infant Church Era. (Insert the name of the key figure on the blank.)

_____ was the key figure of the Infant Church Era.

C. Wheel chart. (Place the name of the key figure on the wheel chart.)

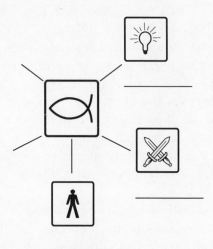

The Adolescent Church Era

I. Review:

Fill in the blanks to bring the wheel chart up to date.

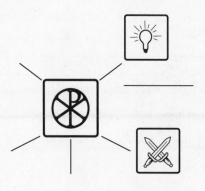

II. Key figure: Augustine of Hippo

Augustine (354–430) was born in Numidia (North Africa) and educated in Carthage. Along with a teaching career, Augustine pursued pleasure. At eighteen, he fathered an illegitimate son. A decade later he moved to Italy, where he came under the teaching of Ambrose, the bishop of Milan.

In 386, Augustine had a profound conversion experience. He returned to North Africa, founded a monastery, and in 396, became the bishop of Hippo. He fought heresies, debated false teachers, arbitrated lawsuits, trained clergy, and ministered to an unlettered congregation, many of whom spoke only Punic, the Phoenician dialect of ancient Carthage.

Augustine was the greatest thinker of the age. He upheld the authority of the church and provided reasoned statements for difficult doctrines, such as the Trinity, grace, and sin. He produced more than one thousand manuscripts, including his classic works *Confessions,* an autobiography, and *The City of God,* a Christian philosophy of history.

Augustine bequeathed a rich legacy to the Medieval Church Period. His writings underscored doctrine. His monastery became the prototype for clerical education, and his treatise, *On Christian Doctrine,* set the guidelines for the twelfth-century European universities.

SUMMARY

_____ was the key figure of the Adolescent Church Era.

III. Summary of other important figures:

1. Athanasius

2. John Chrysostom

3. Jerome

1. Athanasius: The bishop who fought Arianism. Athanasius (c. 296–373) was a clergyman who attended the Council of Nicea. In 328, he became the bishop of Alexandria and devoted his life to fighting Arianism. Athanasius promoted Nicene (anti-Arian) orthodoxy; he stressed the Incarnation, the Trinity, and the work of Christ. Athanasius was exiled five times for his anti-Arian beliefs. He fought the heresy so tenaciously that a slogan was coined: "Athanasius against the world."[4]

Athanasius made several other contributions to the church. He was the first leader to recommend the Psalms for private devotions; his *Easter Letter* was the first document to officially list a twenty-seven-book canon for the New Testament; and his *Life of St. Antony,* a biography about the founder of monasticism, influenced both Jerome and Augustine.

2. John Chrysostom: The preacher known as the "golden-mouthed." John Chrysostom (c. 350–407) was educated in Antioch at the "Harvard" of the empire, a school run by the pagan Libanius, the most famous educator of the era. John became a Christian in his teens. He was ordained a priest in 386 and spent twelve additional years in Antioch, where he became a celebrated preacher. John was charismatic, articulate, and highly principled. In 398, he was appointed the bishop of Constantinople, the most powerful post in the Eastern church.

John rebuked the Christians of Constantinople as he had rebuked the Christians of Antioch. His truthful, sometimes tactless, comments made powerful enemies—including the Empress Eudoxia, the local lax clergy, and a rival bishop. The eloquent John plainly lacked skill in ecclesiastical politics. He was exiled by the emperor and died in 407.

By the sixth century, John was recognized as the greatest preacher in church history and dubbed *chrysostomos,* "the golden-mouthed." He left more than six hundred short sermons (homilies) containing practical applications and pastoral encouragement.

3. Jerome: The biblical scholar of Bethlehem. Jerome (331–420) lived an adventurous life. He traveled widely in Gaul, Greece,

Asia Minor, Syria, Palestine, Egypt, Rome, and Constantinople. He was attracted to asceticism, lived four years as a hermit, mastered Greek and Hebrew, and became the secretary to the bishop of Rome.

In 386, Jerome settled in Bethlehem, where he established a monastery, convents, a church, and a guest house for pilgrims and lived out the last thirty-four years of his life. The bulk of his time was devoted to biblical scholarship. He produced a new Latin translation of the Bible, the Vulgate, which was the greatest literary masterpiece of the Adolescent Church Era.

Jerome also translated some of the apocryphal (extrabiblical) books but denied that they were equal to Scripture. He wrote commentaries, addressed controversial Church issues, and maintained contact by letter with Christians throughout the empire, including Augustine, with whom he corresponded for twenty-five years.

Self-Test

A. Important figures of the Adolescent Church Era. (Identify the key figures from the descriptive statements.)

Augustine   Athanasius   Jerome
John Chrysostom

_____ The greatest preacher in the history of the church.

_____ Settled in Bethlehem and devoted his life to biblical scholarship.

_____ Bishop who fought Arianism.

_____ The greatest thinker of the age.

B. Key figure of the Adolescent Church Era. (Insert the name of the key figure on the blank.)

_____ was the key figure of the Adolescent Church Era.

C. Wheel chart. (Place the name of the key figure on the wheel chart.)

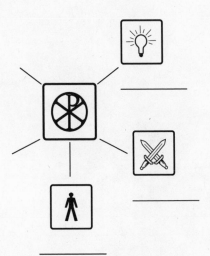

ELEVEN

WRITERS/WRITINGS: ANCIENT CHURCH PERIOD

H arriet Stratemeyer Adams (1894–1982) is not a household name, yet she was one of America's most prolific authors. She wrote several hundred books, and more than 250 million copies of her stories were printed.

With such a publishing record, what is the reason for her obscurity? Mrs. Adams wrote for young people, and she frequently used pseudonyms. For over fifty years, Harriet Adams created the episodes for several popular juvenile series—the Bobbsey Twins, Nancy Drew, Hardy Boys, and Tom Swift.

Unfortunately, many of the writers of the Ancient Church Period are as obscure to us as Mrs. Adams, since the early church writers wrote in languages few moderns ever use. Still, these ancient writers supply the church with invaluable records about its founding beliefs and offer insightful glimpses of early church life. Our study will first examine the key writer or writing of the era and then survey three other important entries. The key writer/writing will appear in a boxed summary statement.

The Infant Church Era

I. Review:

Fill in the blanks to bring the wheel chart up to date.

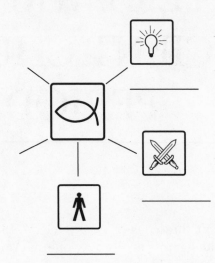

II. Key writing: the New Testament canon

The *New Testament canon* was the technical term for the list of scriptural writings approved by the church. Leaders began developing the canon during the Infant Church Era. The threefold process included the recognition that certain writings were divinely inspired, the scrutiny of individual letters (to verify that they had been written by an apostle or someone close to an apostle and to insure that the teachings met apostolic standards), and finally, official certification.

Developing the New Testament canon was critical. As the early disciples of Christ died, leaders needed an authoritative body of literature to transmit the gospel. Furthermore, heretical claims forced bishops to certify writings. The false teacher, Marcion (c. 140), for example, issued a canon of the New Testament that contained only a skewed version of Luke plus ten Pauline epistles. Finally, because persecution was sometimes tied to yielding the Scriptures, believers had to know which writings to protect.

The New Testament canon existed by the time of Irenaeus (c. 175), but some bishops deliberated over certain disputed books—epistles that were recognized as scriptural but contained "problem areas." For instance, the book of Hebrews was questioned because of its uncertain authorship. The canon was collected and used during the Infant Church Era, but it was not officially approved until the Synod of Carthage in 397.

SUMMARY

The key writing of the Infant Church Era was the _____ _____ _____.

III. Summary of other important writers/writings:

1. *First Apology*

2. Tertullian

3. Origen

1. *First Apology*: A glimpse at a second-century church. *First Apology*, written by Justin Martyr (c. 150), was a plea to Emperor Pius asking for toleration for the Christians. Included in the writing was a detailed description of the rituals and worship of a second-century church:

> At the end of the prayers, we greet one another with a kiss. Then the president of the brethren is brought bread and a cup of wine mixed with water; and he takes them, and offers up praise and glory to the Father of the universe, through the name of the Son and of the Holy Ghost, and gives thanks at considerable length for our being counted worthy to receive these things at his

hands. When he has concluded the prayers and thanksgivings, all the people present express their joyful assent by saying Amen. ("Amen" means "so be it" in Hebrew.) . . . Then those whom we call deacons give to each of those present the bread and wine mixed with water over which the thanksgiving was pronounced, and carry away a portion to those who are absent.

We call this food "Eucharist," which no one is allowed to share unless he or she believes that the things which we teach are true, and has been washed with the washing that is for remission of sins and unto a second birth, and is living as Christ has commanded. For we do not receive them as common bread and common drink; but as Jesus Christ our Saviour, having been made flesh by the word of God, had both flesh and blood for our salvation; similarly we have been taught that the food which is blessed by the word of prayer transmitted from him, and by which our blood and flesh are changed and nourished, is the flesh and blood of that Jesus who was made flesh. For the apostles, in the memoirs called Gospels composed by them, have thus delivered unto us what was enjoined upon them; that Jesus took bread, and when he had given thanks, said, "This do in remembrance of me, this is my body"; and that, in a similar way having taken the cup and given thanks, he said, "This is my blood;" and gave it to them alone.[1]

2. Tertullian: Commentator on Christianity. Tertullian (c. 150–c. 212) was a mysterious figure in church history. Little is known about his private life, his relationship to the local church at Carthage, or his involvement with Montanism—a schismatic movement. Notwithstanding, his writings are without equal. Tertullian, an apologist, a polemicist, and a theologian, was also a colorful, sometimes biting, commentator on church trends. He wrote on martyrdom, prayer and suffering, the role of women in the church, and some of the pagan customs practiced by Christians. Tertullian's writings covered the widest range of subjects of any ancient writer and were studied by all the great Western theologians. One of the most oft-quoted comments in church history was written by Tertullian: "The blood of the martyrs is the seed (of the church)."[2]

3. Origen: Educator and scholar. Origen (c. 185–254) was the most famous Christian of his day; even pagans respected him. He was a brilliant man, head of the Alexandrian catechetical school, and one of the first exegetes (a person who explains and interprets Scripture) in church history. Origen traveled widely, witnessed freely (especially to Jews), and was an accomplished teacher. He produced thousands of writings, including letters, homilies, articles, treatises, and commentaries. Jerome once asked, "Who could ever read all that Origen wrote?"[3]

First Principles and *Hexapla* were two of his significant writings. *First Principles,* the first systematic theology in the church, covered subjects from the doctrine of God to the role of Scripture and gave Christians an intellectual framework on which to base their beliefs.

Hexapla was a parallel translation of six texts of the Old Testament: Hebrew, Greek, the Septuagint, and three other Greek translations. The book was especially useful for Christians who were trying to witness to Jews and pagans.

Self-Test

A. Important writers/writings of the Infant Church Era. (Identify the writer/writing from the descriptive statement.)

Origen   New Testament canon   Tertullian
First Apology

_____ The technical term for the list of approved sacred writings.

_____ The writing that describes early church life.

_____ The writer who produced the *Hexapla.*

_____ The writer who said: "The blood of the martyrs is the seed of the church."

B. The key writing of the Infant Church Era. (Write the name of the key writing on the blanks provided.)

The key writing of the Infant Church Era was the _____ _____ _____.

C. Wheel chart. (Add the name of the key writing to the wheel chart.)

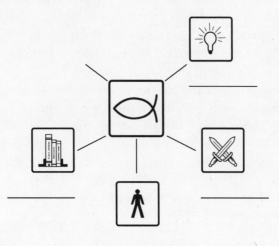

The Adolescent Church Era

I. Review:

Fill in the blanks to bring the wheel chart up to date.

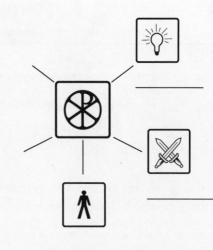

II. Key writing: The Vulgate

The New Testament, written primarily in Greek, was initially shared with Greek-speaking people. As Christianity spread to the Latin-speaking, western regions of the empire, Christians clamored for the Scriptures in Latin. (Butchered translations appeared as early as A.D. 150.)

In 382, when Latin had completely replaced Greek in the Western church, Damascus, the bishop of Rome, commissioned Jerome to produce an accurate Latin translation of the Gospels and the Psalms. Initially, Jerome used the Septuagint, the Greek version of the Old Testament, to translate the Psalms. As he studied, he became convinced that the Old Testament translation should be based on Hebrew, the original language. Jerome's familiarity with Hebrew equipped him to "give my Latin readers the hidden treasures of Hebrew erudition."[4] Jerome ultimately gave his readers the whole Bible.

Jerome's translation, known as the Vulgate (the common version), became the accepted Bible for the next one thousand years, the text of the famed Gutenberg Bible, and the basis for later English translations, like The Wycliffe Bible and The Douai-Reims Bible. Jerome's approach to Bible translation set the precedent for examining the Scriptures in their original languages.

SUMMARY

The key writing of the Adolescent Church Era was the

_____.

III. Summary of other important writings:

1. The *Rule*

2. *Ecclesiastical History*

3. *Confessions*

1. The *Rule*: The pattern for monastic life. The *Rule* was a pattern for monastic life written by Benedict of Nursia (c. 480–c. 547), the founder of the Benedictines and one of the most influential leaders in Western monasticism. The Benedictine *Rule* regulated hundreds of medieval monasteries.

The *Rule* viewed the monastery as a self-sufficient world in which the monks lived a strenuous but not overburdened life. Worship and labor dominated the day. There were seven prayer periods, including a 2:00 A.M. vigil. Monks wove fabric, made clothing, and planted fields. Each monastery had a library, and reading was encouraged, particularly during the winter months. No one could join a Benedictine monastery until he had "tested" the life for a year.

2. *Ecclesiastical History*: The first complete history of the Church. *Ecclesiastical History* was the first exhaustive history of the Church. The book was written by Eusebius (c. 263–c. 339), the bishop of Caesarea (Palestine), who wanted "to record the succession of the holy apostles, together with the times since our Savior."[5] Eusebius wrote about the bishops of the major cities, the false teachers, the tribulations of the Jews, and the martyrdoms of Christians. The *Ecclesiastical History* was originally published around A.D. 303 but was later revised to include the reign of Constantine, a man who was greatly admired by the historian.

Eusebius was not a winsome writer. His book was invaluable, however, because it included long excerpts from other ancient authors whose works have not otherwise survived. The *Ecclesiastical History* earned Eusebius the title "the Father of Church History."

3. *Confessions*: A spiritual autobiography. *Confessions* was the first autobiography ever written. The book describes the spiritual pilgrimage of Augustine of Hippo from his youth to his mid-forties. Although the book reviews the theologian's life, it focuses on God. In fact, much of *Confessions* is rhapsodic prayer.

Augustine, who wrote with incisive emotional honesty, came to Christ late in life and never forgot his spiritual awakening:

Late have I loved Thee whose fairness is so old and yet so new.
Late have I loved Thee. . . . Unlovely I broke upon the loveliness
which Thou hadst fashioned. Thou wert with me and I was not
with Thee. Long was I held from Thee by those things which
without Thee are naught. Thou didst call and cry and burst my
deafness. Thou didst gleam and glow and dispel my blindness.
Thou didst exhale fragrance. I drew breath and I panted after
Thee. I have tasted and do hunger and thirst. Thou hast touched
me and I burned for Thy peace.[6]

The most famous quote from *Confessions* is found in Book I:
"Thou hast made us for thyself, O Lord, and our hearts are restless
until they find their rest in Thee."[7]

Self-Test

A. Important writings of the Adolescent Church Era. (Identify the writing from the descriptive statement.)

The Vulgate   *Confessions*   The *Rule*
Ecclesiastical History

_____ The pattern for monastic life.

_____ Jerome's common or Latin translation
of the Bible.

_____ Augustine's spiritual autobiography.

_____ A record of the church from the time
of Christ through Constantine.

B. Key writing of the Adolescent Church Era. (Write the name of the key writing on the blank provided.)

The key writing of the Adolescent Church Era was the

_____ .

C. Wheel chart. (Add the name of the key writing to the wheel chart.)

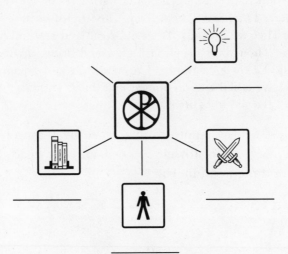

TWELVE

TRENDS: ANCIENT CHURCH PERIOD

W hat do great art, great music, and great literature have in common? Great contrast. Consider the poem, "Swift Things Are Beautiful," by Elizabeth Coatsworth:

Swift things are beautiful:
Swallows and deer,
And lightning that falls
Bright-veined and clear,
Rivers and meteors,
Wind in the wheat,
The strong-withered horse,
The runner's sure feet.
And slow things are beautiful:
The closing of day,
The pause of the wave
That curves downward to spray,
The ember that crumbles,
The opening flower,
And the ox that moves on
In the quiet of power.[1]

Contrast strikes our senses and makes "something" stand out. Who can forget the booming cannons from the "1812 Overture" or the young John Kennedy saluting his slain father?

There was great contrast during the Ancient Church Period as Christianity went from rags to riches. This contrast is clearly seen in the trends that developed during the eras. We will examine the dominant trend for each era and then see how that trend was reflected in church life. Use the boxed summary statements to complete the self-tests.

The Infant Church Era

I. Review:

Fill in the blanks to bring the wheel chart up to date.

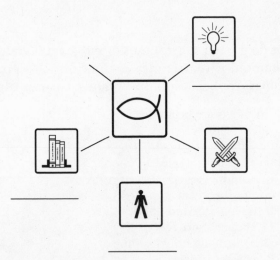

II. Dominant Trend: Informality

Informality dominated the Infant Church Era. In the section that follows, we will examine four areas in the life of the church and see how each developed along simple, casual lines.

SUMMARY

_____ was the dominant trend of the Infant Church Era.

III. Informality Affected:

1. Meeting places

2. Worship/ceremonies

3. Leadership

4. Music and art

1. Meeting places: Homes and catacombs. Because the early Christians expected Christ's imminent return, they were not concerned about buildings. Congregations were small and met in homes. The earliest known church was a converted house located at Dura-Europos on the Euphrates in modern Syria. The building dates to 232 and sheltered about one hundred people.

Christians also met in tombs called catacombs. The most famous catacombs were outside Rome, but catacombs existed in Asia Minor, Malta, North Africa, Paris, and Trier (northeastern Gaul).

2. Worship/ceremonies: Simple rituals. Worship in the early church included sacred readings, instruction, and prayer. Services were conducted in Greek; sermons were extemporaneous. Christians stood with arms uplifted to pray. They memorized and recited simple biblical statements, known as the *Rule of Faith.*

Church ceremonies included baptism, the Lord's Supper, and the laying on of hands to commission leaders. In the New Testament, baptism occurred immediately after conversion, but early church leaders soon established prebaptismal classes, especially for the Gentile converts. Catechumens, people receiving instruction, studied about three years. They were instructed by laymen, although some converts attended schools like the famous catechetical school at Alexandria. Baptism was the believer's initiation into Christianity and occurred at Easter. Initially, only adults were baptized; infant baptism became popular during the third century.

By the second century, worship services were divided into two sections: the synaxis and the Lord's Supper, or Eucharist (*Eucharist* was the Greek term; *Holy Communion* was the Latin term). The synaxis included readings from the Septuagint and the letters of the apostles, hymns, and a sermon. After the synaxis, catechumens were dismissed. Only the baptized remained for the Lord's Supper and the concluding offering, thanksgiving, and benediction.

The laying on of hands, later called ordination, took place during a special dedicatory prayer service. The commissioning was a time for confirming what the Holy Spirit had already revealed to the church, namely that a person was called out for ministry.

The church also celebrated Easter and Pentecost. Easter commemorated the resurrection of Christ and was observed on the first Sunday after Passover. Pentecost, which occurred fifty days after Passover, celebrated the coming of the Holy Spirit.

3. Leadership: The bishop as chief teacher. Although leadership in the Infant Church included the bishop, elders, and deacons, the bishop was the chief teacher. Bishops addressed spiritual matters, but some of the early sermons contained an odd assortment of practical advice:

> Don't cram food into your mouth as if you were packing for a journey. . . . Keep laughter in check. Man is not to laugh all the time because he is a laughing animal any more than a horse is to neigh all the time because he is a neighing animal. . . . If attacked by sneezing, do not startle the company with the explosion.[2]

4. Music and art: Psalm songs and symbols. Songs were based on the Psalms or selected Scripture passages, such as Luke 1:46–

55, the Magnificat. The oldest extrabiblical hymn was the "Shepherd of Eager Youth." The hymn was written around 210 by Clement, the head of the Alexandrian school for catechumens, and was used to instruct converts.

Early Christian art was graffiti—sketches, drawings, and epitaphs that adorned ancient walls and tombs—and symbols, like the ichthus, the cross, and the lamb.

Early Christianity was simple and unstructured. Its spirit was best captured by Clement of Alexandria:

> We cultivate our fields, praising. We sail the seas, humming. Our lives are filled with prayers and praises and Scripture reading before meals and before bed, and even during the night. By this means, we unite ourselves to the heavenly choir.[3]

Self-Test

A. Trends of the Infant Church Era. (Match the terms to the trends described below.)

Meeting places   Leadership   Worship/Ceremonies
Music and art

_____ Psalm songs and symbols.

_____ Homes and catacombs.

_____ Baptism, the Lord's Supper, and commissioning leaders.

_____ The bishop as chief teacher.

B. Dominant trend summary. (Complete the statement.)

_____ was the dominant trend of the Infant Church Era.

C. Wheel chart. (Place the dominant trend on the wheel chart.)

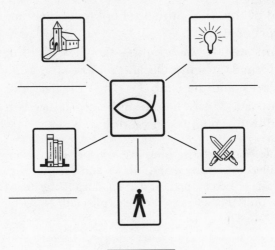

The Adolescent Church Era

I. Review:

Fill in the blanks to bring the wheel chart up to date.

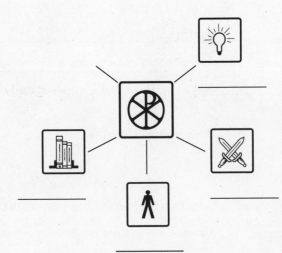

II. Dominant Trend: Formality

In contrast to the Infant Church Era, the Adolescent Church Era was characterized by increasing formality. In the section that follows, we will see the how the Church developed along structured, ritualistic lines.

SUMMARY

_____ was the dominant trend of the Adolescent Church Era.

III. Formality Affected:

1. Meeting places

2. Worship/ceremonies

3. Leadership

4. Music and art

1. Meeting places: The basilica. State sanction of Christianity brought hosts of pagans into the church. Since homes could no longer accommodate the crowds, Constantine chose the basilica, a Roman assembly hall, as the prototype for the church and erected buildings at state expense.

The Christian basilica was rectangular and was divided into three sections by two rows of columns that ran parallel to the longer side of the structure. The choir and fledgling clergy occupied the center section, called the nave. Ordinary worshipers used the two side sections; men and women were separated. An apse, a semicircular niche, adjoined one of the shorter sides. The apse contained a special seat for the bishop, benches for the lesser clergy, a pulpit, and an altar.

Basilicas were functional buildings that quickly became objects of art. One of the most famous basilicas was St. Peter's in Rome, built by Constantine over the traditional site of the apostle's grave.

2. Worship/ceremonies: Formal rituals. Holidays multiplied and ceremonies grew more formal. The church developed a "calendar," honored saints, formulated creeds, wrote liturgies (rites prescribed for public worship), and promoted pilgrimages to the Holy Land. The celebration of Easter expanded to a week and included Palm Sunday, Maundy Thursday, and Good Friday. The pre-Easter period of study and fasting for the catechumens stretched into forty days and became known as Lent.

Pagan influences, such as sun worship, tainted traditions. In 321, Sun-day, named after the unconquered sun, became an official holiday. In 336, Christmas was assigned to December 25, the sun's birthday. Saturnalia, a Roman festival held in December, launched the Christmas gift-giving concept.

3. Leadership: Bureaucracy multiplied. The clergy gained status. Bureaucracy multiplied with the addition of archbishops, metropolitans, and primates. In the West, Leo (440–461) created the papacy with its doctrine, policies, and prerogatives. Ordination grew more formal: new clergy were given gifts of Bibles, chalices (drinking cups for the Eucharist), and vestments (special liturgical clothing). Preaching highlighted worship, and great orators were rewarded with influential assignments. The issue of clerical celibacy, abstaining from sexual intercourse, was debated as some clergy openly maintained illicit relationships.

4. Music and art: Hymns and Byzantine beauty. Ambrose (c. 339–397), the bishop of Milan, was the first leader to promote congregational singing. When Empress Justina tried to transfer a church to an Arian priest, Ambrose and his congregation organized a sit-in. The congregation passed the time by singing hymns with rhyming stanzas. Ambrose, a songwriter, was greatly criticized for the faddish singing, but among Ambrose's later admirers was Augustine, who found consolation in the hymns. Ambrose is called "the Father of Latin hymnody [the history and study of hymn singing and writing]."

In art, the combined elements from the Greek, Roman, Oriental, and Christian cultures produced a distinct style called Byzantine, whose crowning glory was the Church of Hagia Sophia in Constantinople. Hagia Sophia was designed in the shape of a cross, but the roof was its most striking feature. Minor domes covered the ends of the cross, while a magnificent, pillarless dome dominated the intersection. The center dome, which was 180 feet high and supported forty silver chandeliers, added grandeur and spaciousness.

Hagia Sophia showcased the best of Byzantine art. Multicolored marble covered the floors, walls, and colonnades. Stone carvings embellished moldings and cornices. Intricate mosaics adorned the walls. An intricate silver railing protected the apse, which contained the bishop's solid silver chair, a golden altar, and a pulpit inlaid with precious gems.

Hagia Sophia epitomized the formality of the Adolescent Church Era and quickly became known as "the Great Church." At its dedication, the Emperor Justinian exclaimed: "Glory be to God who has thought me worthy to accomplish so great a work! O Solomon! I have vanquished you!"[4]

Self-Test

A. Trends of the Adolescent Church Era. (Match the terms to the trends described below.)

Meeting Places   Leadership   Worship/Ceremonies
Music and Art

_____ Church calendars, pilgrimages, and Easter week.

_____ Ambrose and Hagia Sophia.

_____ Basilicas.

_____ Popes, archbishops, metropolitans, and primates.

B. Dominant trend summary. (Complete the statement.)

_____ was the dominant trend of the Adolescent

Church Era.

C. Wheel chart. (Place the description of the dominant trend on the wheel chart.)

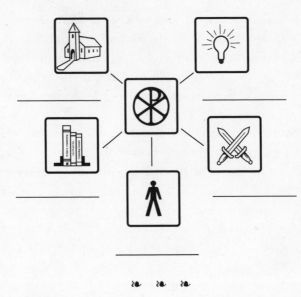

This chapter concludes our study of the Ancient Church Period. We now turn our attention to the Medieval Church Period.

THE MEDIEVAL CHURCH PERIOD

THIRTEEN

GEOGRAPHY: MEDIEVAL CHURCH PERIOD

B etween the end of the Dark Ages (1000) and the Reformation (1517):

- Constantinople was the largest city in the world.
- A journey from Canterbury, England, to Rome took twenty-nine days.
- Slaves still worked in the monasteries.
- A nobleman was distinguished by his signet ring.
- A medieval meal included no coffee or tea.
- Clothes were made to last a lifetime; some were bequeathed as inheritances.
- Pork was commonly eaten, even though it was believed to cause leprosy.
- The ideal medieval woman was tall, slender, and blonde.
- "Mortar boards" were the hats worn by lawyers and doctors.

Since the Middle Ages span nearly one thousand years, medieval geography is vast. The volume of geographical data requires us to be selective. We will focus on five maps which will help us to identify the principal political boundaries and the important places of the two eras.

The Roman Church Era

The Boundaries of Christianity, c. 600

Map I depicts the boundaries of Christianity around 600 and identifies several major barbarian invasions. The lightly shaded area was the jurisdiction of the Roman church. The darker area was controlled by the Eastern church. Label these areas on Map I.

Map I

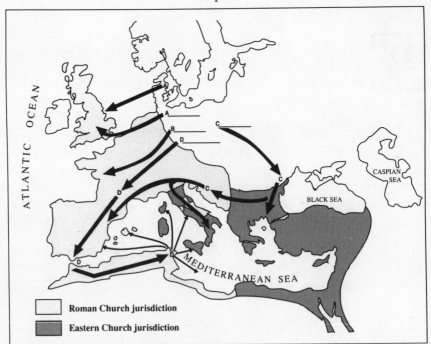

The arrows trace the barbarian invasions. Write the names of the barbarian tribes next to their corresponding letters on Map I.

- The A arrow indicates the conquest of the Angles and Saxons in England.
- The B arrow traces the invasion of the Franks in Gaul.
- The C arrow shows the migration of the Goths throughout southern Europe.
- The D arrow follows the Vandals who settled North Africa and the islands of the western Mediterranean.

The Spread of Islam

The spread of Islam, which transformed the religious complexion of the Mediterranean area, came in three rapid phases. (See Map II.)

Map II

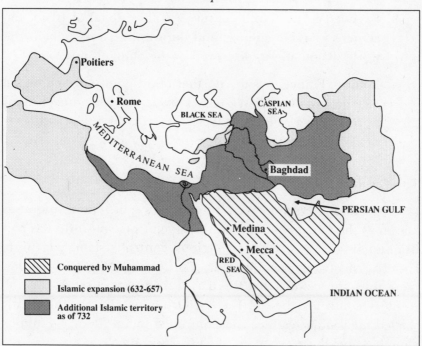

1. The stripped area defines the land conquered under Muhammad (622–632).

2. The lightly shaded area indicates Islamic expansion during the twenty-five years following Muhammad's death (632–657).

3. The darkly shaded area indicates Islamic territory in 732, one hundred years after Muhammad's death.

Four cities were especially important to Islam. After you read each description, underline the name of the city on Map II.

1. Mecca was the birthplace of Muhammad (570–632) and the cradle of the Islamic religion. In July 622, Muhammad fled from Mecca to Medina. His flight was called the *Hegira*.

2. Medina, one of the holy cities of Islam, was the burial place of Muhammad.

3. Baghdad in the tenth century was the capital of Islam, the center of Arabic culture, and the second largest city in the world. Baghdad was destroyed by the Mongols in 1258.

4. Poitiers, France, was the northernmost point reached by the Islamic invaders in Western Europe. In 732, the Muslims were stopped at Poitiers by Charles Martel, the grandfather of Charlemagne.

The Great Schism

In 1054, the Eastern and Western churches split. The division was known as the Great Schism, and the Mediterranean world was partitioned into four areas of religious control: Islam, paganism, Eastern Christianity, and Western Christianity. Map III identifies these four areas. Note that the darkly shaded area represents the territory controlled by the Eastern Orthodox church; the lightly shaded area indicates the land controlled by the Roman Catholic church. Label these two areas of Christian control.

Map III

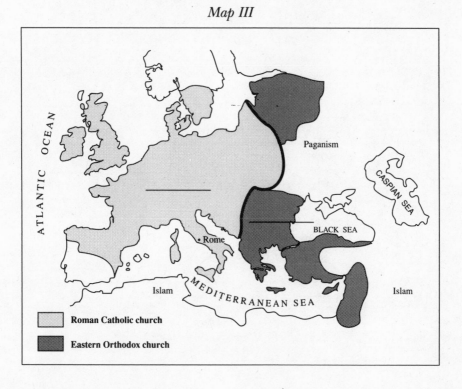

Paganism

CASPIAN SEA

ATLANTIC OCEAN

BLACK SEA

• Rome

Islam

MEDITERRANEAN SEA

Islam

☐ Roman Catholic church

■ Eastern Orthodox church

The Roman Church Era

Let's look at some of the important geographical locations of the Roman Church Era. As you read each description, write the name of the place beside its number/letter on Map IV. Note that the focal region of the Roman Church Era was Western Europe.

Key Cities

- *Rome* (I) was the headquarters of the pope and the Western church.
- *Constantinople* (II) was the capital of the Eastern Empire and the major city of Eastern Christianity.
- *Cordova* (III) was the chief city of Islamic Spain. In 900, the city ranked third in the world behind Constantinople and Baghdad.[1]

Map IV

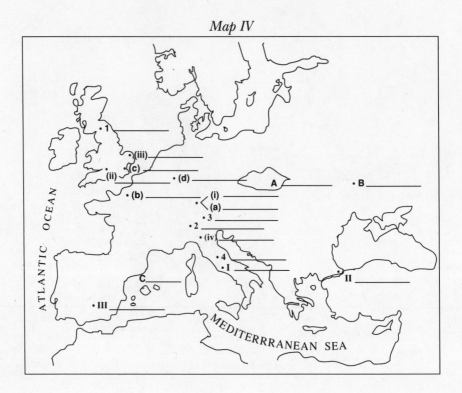

Mission Centers

- *Moravia* (A)—part of modern Czechoslovakia—was a mission field in the ninth century for two Eastern Orthodox monks, Cyril and Methodius.

- *Kiev* (B), the capital of Rus', was ruled by Prince Vladimir, who embraced Christianity in 988. When the prince ordered the baptism of all his subjects, he essentially made Orthodox Christianity the religion of the Ukrainian, Russian, and Byelorussian peoples. The millennial celebration of the great baptism was observed in 1988.

- *Majorca* (C) was the Mediterranean island where the monk Raymond Lull trained missionaries for Muslim countries.

Monasteries

- *Jarrow* (1), a monastery in northern England, was the home of Bede (673–735), the famous scholar and church historian.

- *Cluny* (2), founded in 910, was a French monastery dedicated to reform. At its heyday, the Cluniac order included fifty thousand monks.

- *Clairvaux* (3) was the Cistercian monastery founded in 1115 by Bernard, the most influential monk of the twelfth century.

- *Assisi* (4), in Italy, was the home base of the Franciscan Order.

Gothic Churches

- *Notre Dame de Paris* (a), one of the most widely recognized Gothic cathedrals in the world, was built in Paris in 1235.

- *Notre Dame de Chartres* (b), completed in 1224, is a Gothic cathedral widely admired for its use of diffused light.

- *Westminster Abbey's* (c) interior, rebuilt between 1245–1272, remains a classic example of the early English Gothic style.

- *Cologne Cathedral* (d) is the largest church in Germany. It covers 90,000 square feet and has an interior height of 150 feet. One of its spires is 512 feet tall, half the height of the Eiffel Tower.

Universities

- *The University of Paris* (i) 300was one of Europe's oldest academic institutions. The famed Thomas Aquinas was both a student and a professor at the school.

- *Oxford University* (ii). In 1167, France expelled all foreign students. Many collegians went to England and formed Oxford University.

- *Cambridge University* (iii) was founded around 1200. Among its alumni were some heroes of the English Reformation—William Tyndale, Thomas Cranmer, ThomasCranmer, and Miles Coverdale.

- *Bologna* (iv). Law and medicine dominated the curricula at Bologna in Italy, where women were students by 1215 and held faculty positions by the end of the century. Petrarch (1304–1374), the "Father of Humanism," was a student at Bologna.

The Reformation Church Era

Several places were important during the Reformation Church Era. As you read each description, write the name of the place beside its letter on Map V. Note that the focal region is the Holy Roman Empire.

Map V

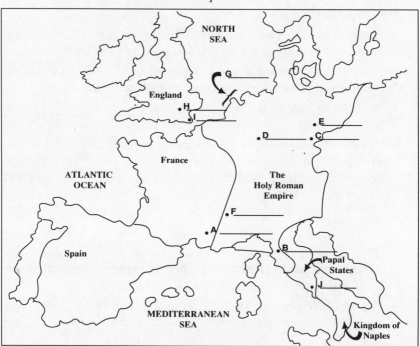

- *Avignon* (A). Avignon was the French residence of the popes during the "Babylonian Captivity" from 1305 to 1377.
- *Florence* (B). The Italian city of Florence was the hub of the Renaissance.

- **Prague** (C). Prague was the city in Bohemia (modern Czecho-slovakia) where the early reformer John Hus (c. 1372–1415) lived and worked.

- **Mainz** (D). Mainz was the German city in the Holy Roman Empire where Gutenberg developed movable metal type, produced the first printed Bible, and launched the printing industry for Western civilization.

- **Wittenberg** (E). Wittenberg was a small town in the German portion of the Holy Roman Empire where Luther posted his Ninety-five Theses. An eyewitness described Wittenberg as "a poor, insignificant town, with little, old, ugly wooden houses."[2] Luther reported the townsfolk were "drunken, rude, and given to reveling" and claimed that civilization ended one mile east of the city.[3]

- **Geneva** (F). Geneva was a Swiss business center in the Holy Roman Empire and a haven for religious exiles. John Calvin devoted his life to organizing the Reformed church in Geneva.

- **Low Countries** (G). The Low Countries were the section of the Holy Roman Empire bordering the North Sea: modern Belgium, Luxembourg, and Holland (the Netherlands). The Low Countries were the "parish" of the itinerant Anabaptist preacher, Menno Simons.

- **London** (H). London was the home of Geoffrey Chaucer (c. 1340–1400) and the starting point for pilgrimages to Canterbury.

- **Canterbury** (I). Canterbury was the site of the shrine of England's most famous saint, Thomas à Becket.

- **The new St. Peter's** (J). The new St. Peter's, begun in 1506 and completed in 1626, was built on the site of the original church. The new St. Peter's, designed in the Italian Renaissance style, is the world's largest church.

SUMMARY

The focal area of the Reformation Church Era was the

_____ _____ _____ .

Self-Test

A. Match the important events and places of the Roman Church Era with their description.

Islam   The Great Schism   Western Europe
Notre Dame de Paris

_____ Gothic cathedral built in 1235.

_____ Transformed the religious complexion of the Mediterranean area.

_____ Focal region of the Roman Church Era.

_____ The Eastern and Western churches split.

B. Match the important events and places of the Reformation Church Era with their description.

Florence   Holy Roman Empire   Wittenberg
Geneva

_____ Focal area of the Reformation Church Era.

_____ Central city of the Italian Renaissance.

_____ Small town where Luther posted his Ninety-five Theses.

_____ City of John Calvin; refuge for exiles.

FOURTEEN

STORY LINE: ROMAN CHURCH ERA

I-5. I-10. I-35. I-80. I-95. These aren't the winning combinations of the latest lottery. These are the names of our nation's great interstate highways. If you live in or near a United States city with a population greater than fifty thousand, you probably travel on at least one interstate.

Interstate highways were the brainchild of the thirty-fourth United States president, Dwight Eisenhower. They were begun in 1956 to link America's major cities in case of national emergency and to carry traffic fast and safely. The United States maintains 42,500 miles of interstate highways. (By comparison, when Jesus was a child, Rome maintained 51,000 miles of paved roads.)

A map of the United States interstate system is impressive. Even-numbered routes travel east and west. Odd-numbered routes run north and south. There are long, straight interstates and short, circular routes with three-digit numbers. Around population centers, interstates cross and diverge like fine cracks in old porcelain.

By 600, there was a great deal of divergence in Christianity. Conflicts between the Roman, Western church and the Greek, Eastern church led to many crisscrossing ideas, alliances, and controversies. Because the Roman church had the greater influence on the course of Western civilization, our study will diverge in that direction. Periodically, however, we will note significant events that occurred in the Greek church.

The Roman Church Era

I. Review:

Fill in the Story of Church History

Period	Era	Date	Epoch	Pivotal Church Figure	Story Line
Ancient Church		30–325	Pentecost Sunday		Bishops _____ the churches as the congregations grew, developed distinct _____ and suffered _____.
	Adolescent			Theologians	Theologians _____ the church, upheld its _____, and continued its _____.
Medieval Church	Roman	600–1300			
	Reformation		Renaissance		
Modern Church		1550–1789		Churchmen	
		1789–present	French Revolution		

II. Story Line Summary:

Monks *tamed* the barbarians, transmitted and *preserved* culture, and *provided* leadership.

SUMMARY

Monks_____ the barbarians, transmitted and_____ culture, and_____ leadership.

III. Expansion:

Four forces that influenced the Roman Church Era were:

1. Gregory the Great

2. Charlemagne

3. Church-state alliance

4. Feudalism

1. Gregory the Great: The first pope of the medieval Roman church. Gregory (c. 540–604) was one of the four Doctors (distinguished leaders) of the Roman church. (The other three were Augustine, Ambrose, and Jerome). Gregory was the first medieval pope (590–604), the first pope to have been a monk, and the first pope to commission monks to evangelize England. Gregory brought the monasteries under the authority of the pope.

Gregory's papacy withstood incredible chaos: plague struck, barbarians ravaged Italy, and the Tiber flooded. Gregory, not the emperor, responded to the tragedies, and in doing so, Gregory made the Roman pope a political figure. The pope managed church revenues and ministered to the needy. He ransomed captives, negotiated peace, and encouraged the fainthearted. Gregory was a humble man who called himself the "servant of the servants of God." He made Rome the proving ground for Augustine's concept of a "Christian commonwealth."

Gregory also shepherded the church at large. He restored orthodox faith in North Africa, asserted the primacy of the Roman see (the jurisdiction of the pope), and welcomed the conversion of Arian Spain. Gregory also popularized medieval folk teachings about purgatory as a place of temporary punishment after death.

2. Charlemagne: The greatest ruler of the Middle Ages. Charlemagne (c. 742–814) would have commanded attention in any age; he stood seven feet tall. He was the son of the famous barbarian warrior, Pepin "the Short," who became king of the Franks and began the Carolingian line of succession. In 756, Pepin made an alliance with the pope that tied the Frankish kingdom of Gaul (modern France, Belgium, parts of Germany, and northern Italy) to the Roman church. This alliance between the barbarian Pepin and the pope greatly offended the Eastern church.

Charlemagne became king in 768 and devoted thirty-four years and fifty-three campaigns to uniting Gaul. His military feats inspired the French epic, *Song of Roland*. Charlemagne was so successful that by the age of sixty-three, he ruled all of the former Western Roman Empire except England, Muslim Spain, and southern Italy. On Christmas Day in 800, Pope Leo crowned Charlemagne "Emperor of the Romans," which made Charlemagne the first medieval Roman emperor. Charlemagne's coronation set the precedent for popes crowning monarchs and resurrected the concept of the Holy Roman Empire, the name given to the western portion of the old Roman Empire because the territory was now ruled by papal support of the monarchy.

Charlemagne united the warring tribes of Gaul with capitularies, or laws, that encouraged individual responsibility. "It is necessary," he wrote, "that every man should seek to the best of his strength and ability to serve God and walk in the way of His precepts; for the Lord Emperor cannot watch over every man in personal discipline."[1] Charlemagne established the practice of tithing to the church, a custom followed throughout medieval times.

To offset paganism, Charlemagne established public education. He enlisted the help of Alcuin, a renown scholar/monk. Alcuin established libraries and trained clergy who, in turn, taught the people. Charlemagne's renewed emphasis on learning was called the Carolingian Renaissance and was one of the few cultural highlights of the Dark Ages.

3. Church-state alliance: The imperfect coalition. When Charlemagne died in 814, his empire was divided among his three sons. The western Frankish kingdom included modern France and Belgium; the eastern section, Germany; the southern segment encompassed northern Italy.

The times were too much for the sons of Charlemagne. Muslims attacked Europe from the south; the Scandinavian Norsemen assaulted the north; and the Magyars (more barbarians) invaded from the east. Feudalism was in its infancy, and papal leadership deteriorated as Roman nobility influenced papal selection. Some of the least effective popes in history ruled between 867–1049. During the tenth century, for instance, the aristocrat, Theophylact, and his daughter, Marozia, manipulated the papacy. Among their papal choices were Sergius III (904–911), Marozia's paramour; John XI (931–935), Marozia's alleged illegitimate son; and John XII (955–964), Marozia's lecherous grandson. Society was in chaos, and the Carolingian line gradually disappeared.

In 962, Otto I was crowned emperor of the eastern Franks, and some stability was restored. The Holy Roman Empire became essentially a German entity, a loose confederation of nobles with wavering allegiances to Otto. Otto cultivated ties with the pope in order to control the nobles. As a result, a tripartite struggle developed between the church, the monarchy, and the nobility. Quarrels centered on the following issues:

• The divorce and remarriage of monarchs
• Jurisdiction of the pope over the courts
• The election of the pope
• The taxation of church property
• Lay investiture (the practice where rulers appointed and installed bishops or abbots and exacted homage from them)

In countries where strong monarchies were developing, for example, England and France, the disputes produced two ideas that significantly altered Western civilization: (1) the recognition of human rights as set forth by the Magna Carta (1215), and (2) representative government, which was played out in councils and parliaments.

4. Feudalism: The framework for medieval society. Feudalism, an elaborate system for safeguarding people and property, originated around the ninth century. Feudalism was a relationship between a lord (a superior) and his vassals (inferiors). Lords provided land (fiefs) for vassals to use. In return, vassals swore obedience to their lord, fought for him, administered his justice, and donated to his causes.

There were class differences among vassals. Vassals of the lowest rank were called serfs. Serfs produced the food and the services needed to sustain society. They were bound to the land and were usually sold with it. Serfs were illiterate people, given more to superstition than true religion. They struggled to eke out a living in spite of flood, plague, and famine. (Sixty famines ravaged France between 970 and 1100.) Serfs paid three annual taxes plus fees to use the lord's grain mill, ovens, winepress, and pasturelands. Serfs fought in wars and tithed their produce and cattle to both the church and their lord.

Vassals of high rank with special training and responsibility were called knights. Knighthood originated with the barbarian concept of fast-moving warriors on horseback. Two inventions allowed knighthood to flourish: stirrups and the iron horseshoe.

Stirrups, introduced by Asian barbarians, gave knights the firm footing necessary to charge lines of foot soldiers. Without stirrups, knights could have easily been toppled from their horses. The iron horseshoe, an invention of the fourth century, enabled horses to maneuver easily on soft or hard ground and to carry heavy weight without damaging their hooves.

Chivalry was the code of behavior for knights. Chivalry required a knight to be loyal to his lord and the church, faithful to the lady he loved, a protector of the helpless, a skilled fighter, and a man committed to truth, justice, and honor. Chivalry introduced a standard for behavior that softened the barbarous conduct of the Dark Ages. Because knights were greatly admired, their code guided civilized behavior.

Self-Test

To check your answers, review the previous pages.

A. Four forces that influenced the Roman Church Era. (Match the force to its descriptive statement.)

Gregory the Great   Charlemagne   Feudalism
Church-state alliance

_____ Affiliation between popes and kings.

_____ "The servant of the servants of God."

_____ The first medieval Roman emperor.

_____ A society of lords and vassals banded together for protection.

B. Story Line Summary. (Fill in the blanks from memory.)

Monks_____ the barbarians, transmitted and_____ culture, and_____ leadership.

C. Arc of Church History. (Fill in the Arc of Church History.)

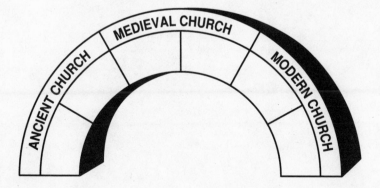

D. Story of Church History. (Fill in the Story of Church History.)

Period	Era	Date	Epoch	Pivotal Church Figure	Story Line
Ancient Church					Bishops _____ the churches as the congregations grew, developed distinct _____, and suffered _____.
					Theologians _____ the church, upheld its _____ , and continued its _____.
Medieval Church					Monks _____ the barbarians, transmitted and _____ culture, and _____ leadership.
Modern Church					

FIFTEEN

STORY LINE: REFORMATION CHURCH ERA

E verything about the Middle Ages seems remote to a twentieth-century observer. But a math exercise may change that perspective.

One of the biggest dates in medieval church history was 1517, the year Martin Luther nailed his theses to the church door in Wittenberg. To learn how many years separate you from this event, take the year you were born and subtract 1517. If, for instance, you were born in 1960, subtract 1517, and you will have a difference of 443 years. That may seem like a long time, but consider how many generations spanned those years.

A generation is the average number of years between the birth of parents and the birth of their offspring. Let's say that one generation is thirty years. Divide thirty into the difference, and you will see the approximate number of generations that separate you from the Reformation. If you were born in 1960, fourteen ancestors stand between you and the aging Martin Luther.

Pondering where that fourteenth ancestor lived, who he was, and how he made a living, helps us relate to the closing era of the Middle Ages. Let's look more closely at the dynamic Reformation Church Era.

The Reformation Church Era

I. Review:

Fill in the Story of Church History.

Period	Era	Date	Epoch	Pivotal Church Figure	Story Line
Ancient Church					Bishops _____ the churches as the congregations grew, developed distinct_____ , and suffered _____ .
					Theologians _____ the church, upheld its _____ , and continued its _____ .
Medieval Church					Monks _____ the barbarians, transmitted and _____ culture, and _____ leadership.
Modern Church					

II. Story Line Summary:

Reformers *questioned* the teachings and *practices* of the church and called for *change*.

SUMMARY

Reformers_____ the teachings and_____
of the church and called for _____.

III. Expansion:

Four forces that influenced the Reformation Church Era were:

1. Renaissance

2. Politics

3. Exploration

4. Inventions

1. Renaissance: Rediscovering roots. Western civilization was the product of Judeo-Christian and Greco-Roman influences. During the Dark Ages, the Judeo-Christian influence dominated society. Between the fourteenth and sixteenth centuries, however, Europeans rediscovered their Greek and Roman roots. Historians call this period of rediscovery the *Renaissance*.

The Renaissance, with its fresh mental outlook, triggered cultural changes that colored the arts, fashioned cities, endowed libraries, established universities (two dozen universities were founded during the fifteenth century), and encouraged invention.

The Renaissance started in Italy with a lawyer named Petrarch (1304–1374), who so loved the classics (the literature of ancient Greece and Rome) that he called Cicero his "father" and Virgil his "brother." Petrarch and his fellow enthusiasts were referred to as *humanists*. Humanists ferreted out the ancient manuscripts that were preserved in the monasteries. They studied the texts and patterned their lives after the teachings of the pagan writers. Humanists gloried in the accomplishments of man.

As the Renaissance spread northward, monks, like Erasmus and Martin Luther, began to study ancient biblical texts. These Christian scholars, who were also called humanists, developed a new appreciation for the content of Scripture and worked eagerly to translate the Bible into native languages. Erasmus wrote:

> I would have those words [the Scriptures] translated into all languages, so that not only Scots and Irishmen, but Turks and Saracens [Arabs] might read them. I long for the plowboy to sing them to himself as he follows the plow, the weaver to hum them to the tune of his shuttle, the traveler to beguile with them the dullness of his journey.[1]

Erasmus published the first Greek New Testament in 1516 at a time when the Latin Vulgate was still the only accepted translation. Erasmus' New Testament influenced later scholars, such as Martin Luther, who translated the Bible into German, and William Tyndale, who translated the Bible into English.

2. Politics: Empires, nations, and rulers. Four significant political developments occurred during the Reformation Church Era: the Eastern Empire fell; Spain became a central power; Europe developed national states; and Charles V became the Holy Roman Emperor. Let's look briefly at each of these developments.

The Fall of the Eastern Empire. During the fourteenth century, the Muslim Ottoman Turks invaded Asia Minor and, within one hundred years, conquered the provinces of the Eastern Empire. In 1453, the Turks took Constantinople, the premiere city of Eastern Christianity, and officially ended the Eastern Roman Empire.

The Eastern church was not destroyed by the Muslim invasion; the patriarch of Constantinople continued as the head of the Greek Orthodox Church. The Muslims, however, exacted heavy fines on the Christians and did not permit them to evangelize.

The Rise of Spain. The marriage of Ferdinand of Aragon to Isabella of Castile in 1469 united Christian Spain under one of the most capable couples in history. In 1492, Ferdinand and Isabella drove the Muslims from Granada after 781 years of occupation, reinstituted the Inquisition, and underwrote the voyage of Columbus.

In 1493, the pope divided the New World between Spain and Portugal. Thereafter, the two countries routinely sent monks to accompany all explorers. While Spain and Portugal were busily planting Catholic missions in the New World, Protestants were debating theology in Europe.

National States. During the sixteenth century, Europe was a patchwork quilt of feudal German and Italian territories tucked around four emerging national states: England, France, Spain, and Portugal. The national states differed from the Holy Roman Empire: each state had consolidated borders, a unifying language, common literature, distinct traditions, and loyal citizenry.

Charles V. Emperor Charles V governed two great kingdoms during his reign (1519–1558). He was heir to the Hapsburg (German) throne, but he was also the grandson of Ferdinand and Isabella of Spain. Charles ruled Spain, the Netherlands, Burgundy (eastern France), the Kingdom of Naples, Sicily, Austria, and Germany and also had rights to Bohemia and Hungary. Charles attempted to unite his kingdom, but his holdings were too scattered. He fought the Turks, the French, the papacy, and the Protestant princes of Germany.

Charles was the ruler who condemned Martin Luther at the Diet of Worms in 1521. While other heretics burned at the stake, Luther was spared because Charles was too preoccupied with politics to quell the religious revolt.

3. Exploration: The new worlds. Feudalism declined as wealth shifted from land to commercial interests. The enterprising Renaissance man looked to the sea and exploration for new products, markets, resources, and revenues.

Spices were highly prized. Martin Luther complained that there was more spice in Germany than grain.[2] Europeans paid extravagant prices for their favorites—cinnamon, cloves, nutmeg, ginger, and pepper. "As dear as pepper" was a common expression.

Spices, along with silk, drugs, and pearls, were bought with precious metals. King Ferdinand balked at importing pepper from

Portugal because it meant releasing silver from Spain's treasury. "Garlic," he protested, "is a perfectly good spice."[3]

Great feats of exploration occurred during the Reformation Church Era. Before Luther was condemned in 1521, Columbus had discovered the West Indies (1492); John Cabot was in Newfoundland (1497); Vasco da Gama had reached India (1498); Balboa had sighted the Pacific (1513); Ponce de Leon had roamed Florida (1513); Cortes had mastered Mexico (1518); and Magellan had sailed around South America (1520).

4. Inventions: Paper, books, and printing. Cheap paper and the invention of printing popularized learning.

When the Muslims conquered Egypt in the seventh century, Europe's papyrus supply was cut off. Scrolls were no longer used, and books were made of costly vellum (lambskin) or common parchment (coarse sheepskin). Skins were cut into rectangular sheets with four, eight, twelve, or sixteen sheets to a folio. Books were expensive; an early medieval book cost between $160 and $200 in 1949 United States currency values.[4] Very few clergy ever owned complete copies of the Bible, and even in the twelfth century, the wealthy had libraries of less than one hundred books.

Papermaking originated in China. In 751, Chinese prisoners in Samarkand (Central Asia) taught the Muslims how to make paper. Paper manufacturing slowly moved westward through Islamic lands before arriving in Europe. Paper mills were established in Baghdad in 794, Cairo in 900, and Islamic Spain in 1150. The first paper mill in Italy came during the fourteenth century as eager university students clamored for notebooks.

The debut of modern printing in 1456 whetted Europe's appetite for reading. By 1500, there were twenty million books in print, and 236 European cities had print shops.[5] Germany led Europe in publishing. But the Venetian printers produced the finest books, and the finest Venetian printer was the Aldine Press. One Swiss scholar wrote to his friend:

> At this very moment a whole wagon load of classics, of the best Aldine [press] editions, has arrived from Venice. Do you want

any? If you do, tell me at once, and send the money, for no sooner is such a freight landed than thirty buyers rise up for each volume, merely asking the price, and tearing one another's eyes out to get hold of them.[6]

Books printed before 1500 were collectively called *incunabula.* They were religious in nature and were written in Latin. During the sixteenth century, the classics and the Reformation writings dominated the book market. Interestingly, science and math books were among the last subjects set to print.

Self-Test

To check your answers, review the previous pages.

A. Four forces that influenced the Reformation Church Era. (Match the force to its descriptive statement.)

Renaissance   Exploration   Politics
Inventions

_____ World-wide search for new markets.

_____ Paper, books, and printing.

_____ Constantinople falls; nations rise.

_____ Renewed interest in Greco-Roman times.

B. Story Line Summary. (Fill in the blanks from memory.)

Reformers_____ the teachings and_____ of the church and called for _____.

C. Arc of Church History. (Fill in the names of the Eras.)

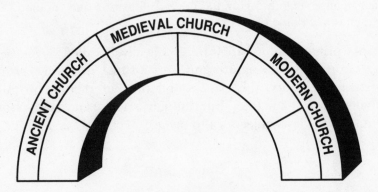

D. Story of Church History. (Fill in the Story of Church History.)

Period	Era	Date	Epoch	Pivotal Church Figure	Story Line
Ancient Church					Bishops _____ the churches as the congregations grew, developed distinct _____, and suffered _____.
					Theologians _____ the church, upheld its _____, and continued its _____.
Medieval Church					Monks _____ the barbarians, transmitted and _____ culture, and _____ leadership.
					Reformers _____ the teachings and _____ of the church and called for _____.
Modern Church					

SIXTEEN

HEADLINES: MEDIEVAL CHURCH PERIOD

Mention *The Times, The News,* or *The Journal,* and modern Americans think "newspaper." But it was not so with the early American colonists. Prior to the Revolutionary War, many of America's thirty-seven newspapers were "gazettes," for example, *The Boston Gazette, The New York Gazette,* and *The Virginia Gazette.*

The word *gazette* originated with the medieval news sheet, the forerunner of the modern newspaper. The news sheet, which appeared around 1513, was like a pamphlet. One of the most famous news sheets was *Notize Scritte,* published in Venice in 1566. The *Notize Scritte* cost a *gazetta,* a small Italian coin, and soon the coin became associated with the news sheet.

Our "gazette" of the Medieval Church Period unfolds on the following pages. It includes typical articles on culture, health, manners, and people and sheds light on a few of the issues which faced medieval Christians.

■ PERSPECTIVE

A LIGHT IN THE DARK AGES

Dateline: Europe; A.D. 1000. Most of medieval Europe staggers under the quadruple hit of barbarians, plague, famine, and war, but the Dark Ages never darkens Spain!

Spain, in A.D. 1000, sparkles. It is modern, sophisticated, and locked on progress, thanks largely to the Muslims, who invaded in 711 and gently nurtured the culture.

As the western frontier of the Islamic Empire, Spain is a chamber of commerce dream: adorned with miles of paved, lighted roads and raised sidewalks, schools, hospitals, seventy public libraries, a postal system, and a merchant fleet of one thousand ships. Stunning cities, like Cordova, Seville, and Granada, showcase Moorish (Arab-Berber) life. Cordova, the urban crown jewel, glistens with opulent cupolas and gilded minarets and lists among its architecture: 200,077 houses, 60,300 palaces, 600 mosques, and 700 public baths.[1]

Moorish society blends Islam with Christian and Jewish influences. Muslims and Christians intermarry and frequently celebrate the holydays of both faiths. Christians are relatively free to worship, but caliphs, the temporal and spiritual Islamic leaders of the regions, keep a close eye on the church. Christian clergy are routinely ridiculed; Church properties confiscated; and evangelism restricted.

The Jews, who aided the invading Muslims, thrive. After the Islamic conquest, fifty thousand Jews migrated to Spain from Africa and Asia and adopted the dress, language, and customs of the Arabs. [2]

Jews excel in scholarship, finance, agriculture, and the professions. Several are court physicians. The Jewish scholar, Hasdai ibn Shaprut (915–970), became prime minister under Caliph Hakam II (961–976) and directed national policy.

Education is highly prized, and book collecting is a mania. Among the Arabs, individual "princes ... in the tenth century might own as many books as could ... be found in all the libraries of Europe combined." [3] The renowned University of Cordova revels in its philosophers, translators, historians, poets, grammarians, anthologists, geographers, jurists, lexicographers, and encyclopedists.

Agriculture prospers. Muslim Spain introduces Christian Europe to maize, rice, sugar, cotton, buckwheat, spinach, and asparagus. Vineyards, groves, and orchards produce a startling variety of fruits, including lemons, dates, cherries, peaches, apricots, oranges, quince, and grapefruit.

Creativity abounds. Ibn Firnas of Cordova invented spectacles, complex chronometers, and a flying machine.[4] (The first European to be credited with the invention of spectacles was Salvino d'Amarto, who died in 1317.[5]) In dozens of areas—from foods and medicines to textiles and maritime codes—Muslim advances spill over into Christendom and bequeath a rich legacy of words: *algebra, Arabic numerals, zero, syrup, sherbet, elixir, satin, damask, muslin, velvet, chess, mattress, sofa, divan, azure, arabesque, bazaar, caravan, almanac, magazine, admiral, barge,* and *sloop.*

The Dark Ages may have dealt Western civilization a staggering blow, but Islamic Spain is stockpiling rich kernels of culture that await germination in Europe. ■

HEALTH

THE MACABRE MIDDLE AGES

Dateline: Europe; A.D. 1352. Europeans hide and pray as the Black Plague continues to stalk urban centers across the continent. After five unabated years of death and destruction, officials offer little hope that the disease has run its course.

Authorities compare the current Black Plague to the first Great Plague of 541 and note several similarities. Both plagues broke out in Constantinople and moved westward through the Balkan peninsula into Italy, France, Spain, and England. Both plagues killed large portions of the population. At the height of the Great Plague, ten thousand people died per day in Constantinople.[6] The death toll from the Black Plague now stands at twenty-five million, and large cities, overwhelmed by dead bodies, have dug "plague pits" to accommodate corpses.[7]

The Great Plague of 541 was followed by fourteen successive epidemics that killed a total of forty million people over a two-hundred-year span.[8] As port cities in the Mediterranean stagger under repeated outbreaks, fear mounts

that the Black Plague will follow a similar pattern.

No segment of society is immune from the plague, which has killed both popes and peasants. Hardest hit are the poor and the physicians and clergy who care for them. Of the 375 bishops alive in 1348, 207 were dead the next year.[9] The symptoms of this rampant disease are even known to children, who chant as they play: Ring around the rosies \ A pocket full of posies \ Achoo! Achoo! \ We all fall down.

The "ring" refers to a red rash that normally surrounds the tender lymphatic swellings, called *buboes,* characteristically located in the groin or armpit areas. During the Great Plague, Procopius, the court historian to Emperor Justinian, wrote, "The bodies of the sick were covered with black pustules [buboes] ... the symptoms of immediate death."[10]

The jingle's "pocket full of posies" are the flowers, herbs, or spices used by caretakers to dispel the sickening odors. "Achoo!" cues listeners to the sneezing, fever, and chills, the telling prelude to the final stage—falling down dead. Few victims last more than five days; many succumb in three.

Survivors tell sad tales. One Italian wrote: "Father abandoned child, wife husband, one brother another.... And I, Agnolo di Tura ... buried my five children with my own hands."[11]

Fear and panic reign. "So many died," said an eyewitness, "that all believed that it was the end of the world."[12] People struggling to find answers blame God, each other, a conjunction of the planets, and "corrupt vapors." Many cling to superstition or charge scapegoats—lepers and Jews—with dastardly deeds like poisoning the water. Jews in France were dragged from their homes in 1348 and burned. German Jews have been murdered in similar attacks. At least six thousand Jews died in Mainz; three thousand in Erfurt.[13] So common is the practice of executing Jews for causing the plague that one thing is sure: when the plague does subside, there will be few Jews left in Europe. ■

LIFE

ON THE SOCIAL SCENE

Dateline: Europe; A.D. 1530. It's happened again! For the second time in two years, a book on etiquette has topped the best-seller list.

In 1528, Count Baldassare Castiglione (1478–1529) served up *The Courtier,* the first blockbuster masterpiece on manners, and hungry readers promptly, but politely, gobbled it up. *The Courtier,* a series of dialogues about the training of medieval gentlemen and ladies, offered a philosophy of the cultured life that has struck a social chord among thousands of European adults.

Now, Erasmus, the famed scholar, cleric, and Bible translator, has targeted children. Erasmus's new handbook is called *On Civility in Children.* Critics and parents have given the guidelines rave notices; children are less enthusiastic. Plans, however, are already being made to incorporate the book into the regular school curriculum.

The books by Castiglione and Erasmus reflect a growing trend that began during feudalism, when medieval yuppies first gained access to royal courts and needed to know how to act at feasts, falconries, and festivals. During the twelfth and thirteenth centuries, etiquette books began to appear. Many were written by clergy, the manners mongers of the courts, who carefully penned the principles of deportment called *courtoisie*. (*Courtoisie* has given us the English word *courtesy*.) The etiquette experts relentlessly emphasized table manners and personal hygiene. Here are some thirteenth-century *courtoisies*:

- A number of people gnaw a bone and then put it back in the dish—this is a serious offense.

- Refrain from falling upon the dish like a swine while eating, snorting disgustingly, and smacking the lips.

- When you blow your nose or cough, turn round so that nothing falls on the table.[14]

For several centuries, until the publication of *The Courtier,* the general population paid little attention to etiquette. You could always tell the lower classes, though, because they ate their food wholehandedly, while aristocrats partook

their meals with the thumb, index, and middle fingers. Judging from some of the current advice Erasmus has given to the children, table manners and personal hygiene still need attention. Here are some of the monk's suggestions:

- If you cannot swallow a piece of food, turn round discreetly and throw it somewhere.

- Do not be afraid of vomiting if you must; for it is not vomiting but holding the vomit in your throat that is foul.

- You should not offer your handkerchief to anyone unless it has been freshly washed. Nor is it seemly, after wiping your nose, to spread out your handkerchief and peer into it as if pearls and rubies might have fallen out of your head.[15] ∎

PEOPLE

THE MONGOL MOGULS

Dateline: Rome; A.D. 1270. As reports continue to circulate that the Kublai Khan (1216–1294) has come to power in Mongolia, the Islamic Empire and Latin Christendom brace, waiting for the inevitable assaults. Both have been invaded by Khan-led Mongols before, and too many in the West remember too much about the bel-

ligerent, robust Mongolians who, according to the papal envoy, Giovanni de Piano Carpini, wore oxhides and ate "anything edible, even lice."[16]

Unless Mongol military strategy has changed drastically, Westerners face a grim prospect: annihilation. Mongol strategy translates into total domination. Mongols leave their victims no opportunity for retaliation and frequently leave no victims alive at all! They burn; they pillage; they rape; they slaughter. Mongols care nothing about cultivating the culture.

The current prospect of a Mongol invasion terrifies Muslims and Christians alike. Khan, in fact, has become the most feared name of the century. He gets a lot of respect, thanks to Genghis Khan (1167–1227), who founded the dynasty in 1206.

Genghis was the first Mongol to shape the fiercely independent nomadic tribes of Central Asia into a disciplined fighting unit. The Mongols were known for their ability to travel fast and far. They attacked North China and, although outnumbered, eventually captured Peking. From the Chinese campaign, Khan learned the art of siege warfare, the effectiveness of gunpowder, and the stratagem of paying tribute.

Khan learned his lessons well and turned his attention westward, conquering much of the eastern Islamic Empire (Iran, Afghanistan, and a portion of northern India). At his death in 1227, the kingdom of Genghis Khan stretched from the Pacific Ocean to the Caspian Sea.

Ogdai, the Great Khan, the successor and son of Genghis Khan, began a second wave of conquests. Mongol hordes pushed into Russia and then into Eastern Europe, defeating, almost at will, the knights of Poland, Hungary, and Germany. Western Europe was doomed, but the Great Khan died suddenly, and the Mongols retreated.

Recent rumors of another great Khan leader, the Kublai Khan, have multiplied with the return from the Far East of two Venetian merchants, Niccolo and Maffeo Polo. The Polos claim to have been in the court of the Kublai Khan and identify the new ruler as the grandson of the Genghis Khan.

The Polo brothers, who have traveled extensively in the Far East, maintain that the Kublai Khan has moved his capital from Mongolia to China and presides over a magnificent court. The merchants believe that the intentions of the Kublai Khan toward Latin Christendom and the Islamic Empire are friendly. The Polos describe the Kublai Khan as a well-educated chieftain, a man who is curious about religion and who is interested in both the Christian and Muslim faiths. On behalf of the Kublai Khan, the Polos have asked the pope to send missionaries to China. A spokesman for Gregory X has confirmed that the request will be honored.

Meanwhile, westerners look toward the East with a mixture of fear and awe, awaiting the next move of the Kublai Khan. ∎

Self-Test

A. Complete the Arc of Church History.

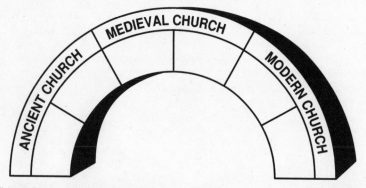

B. Complete the Story of Church History.

Period	Era	Date	Epoch	Pivotal Church Figure	Story Line
Ancient Church					Bishops _____ the churches as the congregations grew, developed distinct _____ , and suffered _____.
					Theologians _____ the church, upheld its _____, and continued its _____.
Medieval Church					Monks _____ the barbarians, transmitted and _____ culture, and _____ leadership.
					Reformers _____ the teachings and _____ of the church and called for _____.
Modern Church					

ҙ   ҙ   ҙ

Tomorrow, we will survey some of the great concepts of the Medieval Church Period.

SEVENTEEN

CONCEPTS: MEDIEVAL CHURCH PERIOD

L et's take a test!

1. Who wrote the *Communist Manifesto*?

2. What was the Cold War?

3. Who led the Protestant Reformation?

These questions are part of a basic history quiz recently given to high school students in Alabama. Here are some of the responses:

1. Thomas Jefferson wrote the *Communist Manifesto*.

2. The Cold War was a big wintertime battle.

3. Jim Bakker led the Protestant Reformation.

The responses may cause us to smile, but there was nothing amusing about the final results: test scores were discouragingly low. What's worse, they reflect the national trend. In the eighties, Americans flunked geography. In the nineties, it's history.

Our basic survey of the Medieval Church Period includes the Protestant Reformation (and tells you who really did lead the movement!) and also examines other important medieval concepts, such as the papacy, monasticism, and the Crusades.

The Roman Church Era

I. The Outstanding Concept: The Papacy

Originally, all of the bishops in the Western church were referred to as "pope." The term, however, gradually became the exclusive title of the bishop of Rome, and his office became known as the papacy. During the Middle Ages, popes slowly garnered the power to transform the papacy from a spiritual office to the highest authority in Western civilization. The papacy reached its apex about 1200. Here are four of the popes who made it happen:

1. Leo the Great (440–461) was technically the first pope. He used Scripture (Matthew 16:18–19 and John 21:15–17) and the Roman law of inheritance to firmly establish the primacy of the bishop of Rome.

2. Gregory the Great (590–604) fought the barbarians and became ruler of Italy. Gregory established the pope as a political figure with temporal responsibilities; from his rule forward, the Roman church functioned independently from the Eastern church, although still bound by ties of protocol.

3. Gregory VII (1073–1085), also called Hildebrand, was an aggressive reform pope who sought to establish papal control over the nobility. Gregory prohibited lay investiture and reserved the right to "free subjects from allegiance to an unjust ruler."

4. Innocent III (1198–1216) was the most powerful pope in church history. He enforced policies and established practices that brought the papacy to its zenith.

SUMMARY

The_____ was the outstanding concept of the Roman Church Era.

II. Summary of Other Important Concepts:

1. Medieval monasticism

2. Crusades

3. Universities/scholasticism

1. Medieval monasticism: The channel for reform. The rise of the papacy in the eleventh century stemmed from broad-based reform movements that swept the monasteries during the tenth century. These reform movements created new monastic orders that supported papal programs. Here are four of the important orders:

1. Cluniacs (910) were monks attached to the French abbey of Cluny and were free from all lay control. Cluny's constituent monasteries were under one central abbot who reported directly to the pope. By the twelfth century, the abbot of Cluny controlled 1100 communities—all loyal to the pope. Cluniacs devoted themselves to formal worship. They were able administrators and dedicated reformers who tried to correct abuses, such as simony (the practice of buying and selling church offices) and nepotism (appointing relatives to church offices).

2. Cistercians (1098) were strict, primitive, reformed Benedictines who accepted no feudal incomes. Their monasteries were located in desolate places. Their monks came from peasant backgrounds. Cistercians were basic, no-frills monks who became leading agricultural pioneers.

3. Franciscans (1210) were one of the two great orders of friars. They were known for their preaching, missionary activities, and social work. The Franciscans were organized by Francis of Assisi and initially owned neither communal nor personal property. Franciscans were mendicants (beggars).

4. Dominicans (1215), the second great order of friars, were dedicated to teaching and preaching. Dominicans opposed heresy and quickly became known as the "watchdogs of the Lord." Many Dominicans served as judges in the Inquisition.

2. Crusades: The papal call to arms. The Crusades were militant pilgrimages undertaken by Western Christians to free the Holy Land from Muslim control. The Crusades were organized by the pope, who promised potential warriors *indulgences* in exchange for their services. An indulgence, a pardon from sin granted by the church, supposedly helped a Christian attain heaven quickly by decreasing the time spent in purgatory.

Seven crusades occurred between 1096 and 1291. The First Crusade (1096–1099) brought the most glory. Nearly five thousand knights captured Jerusalem and established Latin states along the coasts of Syria and Palestine. But the victories were short-lived. Succeeding crusades failed to secure the Holy Land and found crusaders committing atrocities against Eastern Christians, Muslims, and Jews.

3. Universities/scholasticism: The renewal of medieval minds. After the Dark Ages, education shifted to the universities. Peter Abelard (1079–1142), a controversial teacher who encouraged his students to question and doubt, was a pioneer of the concept of higher education. Among the first universities were Paris, Oxford, Cambridge, and Bologna. Undergraduates mastered the liberal arts: arithmetic, geometry, astronomy, music, grammar, logic (philosophy), and rhetoric. Graduates studied theology, law, and medicine.

Scholasticism was the philosophical mind-set of the medieval educators, who were known as schoolmen. Schoolmen attempted to reconcile reason and faith and to arrange the teachings of the church in a logical system. Schoolmen asked questions and relied on Aristotle, the Scriptures, and Augustine of Hippo for the answers. The most celebrated schoolman was Thomas Aquinas.

Self-Test

A. The important concepts of the Roman Church Era. (Match the concepts to the descriptions below.)

The papacy   Medieval monasticism   Crusades
Scholasticism

_____ The office of the bishop of Rome.

_____ Schoolmen's attempts to reconcile faith and reason.

_____ Military campaigns to free the Holy Land from Islamic control.

_____ Reform-minded orders that supported the pope.

B. The outstanding concept of the Roman Church Era. (Insert the name of the outstanding concept on the blank.)

The_____ was the outstanding concept of the Roman Church Era.

C. Wheel chart. (Place the name of the outstanding concept on the wheel chart.)

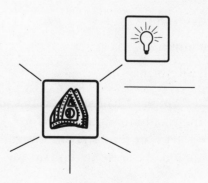

The Reformation Church Era

I. The Outstanding Concept: The Reformation

The Reformation was an attempt to revitalize the Roman Catholic church. Martin Luther, a German monk, has been credited with starting the Reformation by posting a document, the Ninety-five Theses, on a church door in Wittenberg on October 31, 1517.

Luther's initial concern was the sale of indulgences—the practice by which Christians paid for the pardons that had earlier been given to the crusaders. Luther's ire was directed toward John Tetzel, a Dominican, who was selling indulgences to finance St. Peter's in Rome. Tetzel's sales pitch was: "As soon as the coin in the coffer rings, the soul from purgatory springs."[1]

Underlying Luther's concerns were fundamental church issues involving authority, sin, salvation, and repentance. Resolving these concerns eventually split Western Christianity.

SUMMARY

The_____ was the outstanding concept of the Reformation Church Era.

II. Summary of other important concepts:

1. Early Reformers

2. Protestantism

3. Counter-Reformation

1. Early Reformers: Challengers to the status quo. Prior to Luther, several men had attempted to reform the church. John Wycliffe (c. 1330–1384), an Englishman, was called the "Morning Star of the Reformation" because he upheld the authority of Scripture and questioned the doctrine of transubstantiation—the teaching that Christ was physically present in the Communion elements.

John Hus (c. 1372–1415) was a Bohemian priest who upheld the authority of Scripture, condemned the sale of indulgences, and fought ecclesiastical corruption. Hus was declared a heretic and executed. His followers, the Hussites, were alternately persecuted and tolerated; many survived to support the Reformation.

Girolamo Savonarola (1452–1498) was an electrifying Dominican preacher who helped transform Florence, Italy, from a corrupt city to a quasi-monastic community. In the process, Savonarola made mortal enemies, including Pope Alexander VI, who excommunicated the "meddlesome friar" and eventually had him tortured and executed.

The Brethren of the Common Life was a monastic community within the Catholic church that encouraged personal piety and social involvement. The Brethren devoted themselves to education; they were skilled copyists, writers, printers, and teachers. Erasmus, Martin Luther, and Thomas a Kempis were schooled by the Brethren.

2. Protestantism: A new label for old beliefs. At the Diet of Speyer in 1529, Emperor Charles V ordered Luther's religious reform movement stopped. Several German princes who protested were labeled "Protestants," and the name stuck.

Among the Protestants, four distinct traditions developed: the Lutheran, the Reformed, the Anglican, and the Anabaptist. Although rituals differed, Protestants shared three common beliefs:

1. Salvation is by grace through faith in Jesus Christ.

2. Religious authority ultimately lies with Scripture.

3. The church is a priesthood of believers.

3. Counter-Reformation: Roman Catholicism responds. The Counter-Reformation was the Catholic response to the Protestant call for reform. The Counter-Reformation was led by Pope Paul III (1534–1549), who acknowledged "that our Holy Mother the Church . . . has been so changed that she seems to have no tokens of her evangelical character; and no trace can be found in her of humility, temperance, continence, and apostolic strength."[2]

Catholic reform came in different ways. There was an increased desire for personal spirituality, as exemplified by Teresa of Avila, the Spanish mystic. Missionary ventures multiplied. Francis Xavier (1506–1552) was credited with the conversions of more than seven hundred thousand Asians. Finally, new monastic orders were created. The Jesuits, for example, presented reformed Catholic theology through education. By 1640, the Jesuits had established four hundred colleges.

Self-Test

A. The important concepts of the Reformation Church Era. (Match the concepts to the descriptions below.)

Early reformers   The Reformation   Protestantism
Counter-Reformation

_____ The renewal movement led by Martin Luther.

_____ The Catholic response to the Protestant call for reform.

_____ Wycliffe, Hus, and Savonarola.

_____ The tradition that espoused salvation by grace, the authority of Scripture, and the priesthood of believers.

B. The outstanding concept of the Reformation Church Era. (Insert the name of the outstanding concept on the blank.)

The_____ was the great concept of the Reformation Church Era.

C. Wheel chart. (Place the name of the outstanding concept on the wheel chart.)

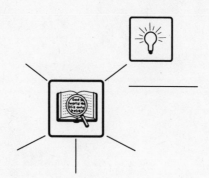

EIGHTEEN

FOES: MEDIEVAL CHURCH PERIOD

Mark Twain once sued a rival publisher who printed *Huckleberry Finn* before Twain's company could issue it. When Judge Le Baron Colt ruled against Twain, the writer was enraged.

> The judge has allowed the defendant to sell property which does not belong to him but to me, property which he has not bought and I have not sold.
>
> Therefore, under this same ruling I am now advertising the judge's homestead for sale; and if I make as good a sum out of it as I expect, I shall go on and sell the rest of his property.[1]

Conflict is a part of every time; church history is no exception. Our study of the Medieval Church Period looks at some of the people and ideas that troubled the church.

The Roman Church Era

I. Review:

Fill in the wheel chart to bring the era up to date.

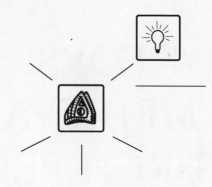

II. The major foe: Islam

While Gregory was shaping the medieval papacy, Islam was being birthed in far-off Arabia. In less than one hundred years, the Muslim faith supplanted Christianity in the Middle East, North Africa, and Spain.

Here are some significant facts about Islam:

1. Founded in 622 by Muhammad.

2. *Islam* means "submission to Allah (God)."

3. The Koran was the sacred book of Islam.

4. Pillars of Islam:
   - "There is no god but Allah, and Muhammad is His prophet."
   - Prayer, five times a day.
   - Fasting, especially during the holy month of Ramadan.
   - Almsgiving to the needy.
   - Pilgrimage to Mecca.

Islam united Arabs in a brotherhood of faith around the *jihad,* or "holy war." Conquered pagans (polytheists) accepted Islam or died; Jews and Christians (monotheists) were allowed to continue in their faith but were assessed a special tax.

Medieval Christians considered the Muslims "infidels" and were repulsed by the Muslim occupation of any Christian land. In the late eleventh century, a Muslim attack on the Byzantine Empire triggered the First Crusade.

SUMMARY

The major foe of the Roman Church Era was _____ .

III. Summary of the Other Foes:

1. The Iconoclastic Controversy

2. The Great Schism

3. The Inquisition

1. The Iconoclastic Controversy: Icons and worship. Icons were flat images of Christ, Mary, and other saints that were painted (the technical term is *written*) on wood or worked in ivory or mosaic. Icons were used in the Greek church to stimulate worship. They were called "windows to heaven" and were venerated as reminders of the Incarnation.[2] One bishop summarized their importance: "They [icons] are the books of the unlearned. The man who cannot read sees the image and his mind is lifted up from that image to that for which it stands."[3]

Because uneducated people began using icons in superstitious ways, iconoclasts (image breakers) wanted to abolish the images. The dispute came to a head in 730, when Emperor Leo III banned icons from public places, and the masses rioted in Constantinople. The iconoclasts retaliated. Persecution broke out and continued for years. Finally, the Council of Nicea in 787 restored the icons and outlined guidelines for their use, but it was not until 843 that the iconoclastic controversy was completely put to rest.

2. The Great Schism: The Roman and Greek churches separate. In 1054, the Greek and Roman churches separated. The division, called the Great Schism, resulted from several factors. In particular, the Greek church objected to the addition of the *filioque* ("and the Son") clause in the Nicene Creed. Originally, the Nicene Creed had stated: "the Holy Ghost . . . proceedeth from the Father." But, in 589, the Roman church inserted "proceedeth from the Father *and the Son.*" When the Greeks maintained that the Holy Spirit proceeded not *from* but *through* the Son, lines were drawn.

Politics was the straw that broke church unity's back. In 1054, the Roman church, awakening from the Dark Ages, ruled over warring, uncouth people and selected its leaders from among the barbarians. As such, the Roman church was an embarrassment to the Greek church, which was enjoying a resurgence of Byzantine glory. The Greek church had just recaptured territory from the Muslims, reestablished its authority in southern Italy (which confused the Italian Christians who were used to Western leadership), revitalized its art and literature, and extended its influence to the Slavs. In April 1054, while trying to settle the issue of leadership in southern Italy, Roman and Greek church diplomats mutually excommunicated one another, and the Great Schism was accomplished.

3. The Inquisition: The hunt for heretics. Medieval society believed that the church had been established by God and that anyone who attacked Christianity was a heretic. During the Dark Ages, heresy was punished by excommunication. As heretics became harder to control, corrective measures became more drastic.

The Inquisition was a church court which tried accused heretics. The court concept was based on Roman tradition and claimed biblical precedent (Deuteronomy 13:1–9; 17:2–7). Court judges, called inquisitors, were usually Dominicans or Franciscans. Judges were not impartial but served to exact punishment on "the enemies of Christ."

By 1232, standard inquisitorial procedures were in place. Suspected heretics were given opportunities to recant. Those who confessed performed a penance, but the less compliant faced trial, jail, or more likely, execution. Because the church refused to administer the death sentence (the "church shrinks from blood"), the state executed heretics, usually by burning them at the stake. While the Inquisition controlled heretics, it unnecessarily repressed many legitimate concerns.

Self-Test

A. Famous foes of the Roman Church Era. (Write the foe next to the appropriate statement.)

Islam   Iconoclastic Controversy   Inquisition
Great Schism

_____ A dispute over the images used in worship.

_____ A church court which tried accused heretics.

_____ Separation of the Greek and Roman churches in 1054.

_____ Monotheistic faith guided by the Koran.

B. Major foe of the Roman Church Era. (Insert the name of the major foe on the blank below.)

_____ was the major foe of the Roman Church Era.

C. Wheel chart. (Place the name of the major foe on the wheel chart.)

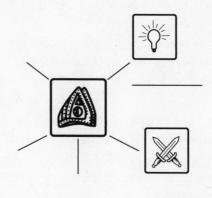

The Reformation Church Era

I. Review:

Fill in the wheel chart to bring the era up to date.

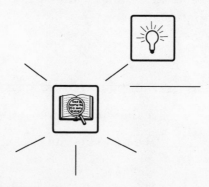

II. The major foe: Papal decline

Papal decline describes a condition that began around 1300 and continued throughout the Reformation Church Era. The section below examines four areas affected by papal decline and places them in a historical context.

SUMMARY

The major foe of the Reformation Church Era was_____
_____.

III. Summary of other foes:

1. The "Babylonian Captivity"

2. The Papal Schism

3. Renaissance popes

4. Rigid practices

1. The "Babylonian Captivity" (1305–1377): The era of French popes. The "Babylonian Captivity" refers to the seventy-year period when all popes were French and ruled from Avignon, France. The Captivity was triggered by a violent conflict between Pope Boniface VIII and the French king, Philip IV, over papal jurisdiction. When Boniface died in 1303, Philip's troubles seemed over. However, to ensure the election of a cooperative pope, Philip persuaded the College of Cardinals to elect a French pope, Clement V. Fearing the Italians, Clement refused to serve in Rome and moved the papacy to Avignon, France. All Christendom protested, but the papacy remained in France.

The "Babylonian Captivity" disrupted the church because close papal ties with France gave the appearance of partiality toward that country and bred ill-will. Furthermore, the extravagances of the Captivity popes, along with their excessive taxes, intensified the cries for reform.

2. Papal Schism (1378–1417): The era of multiple popes. The papacy had scarcely returned to Rome when a new crack appeared in church leadership. In 1378, Urban VI was elected pope. Urban was so obnoxious that within a few months he alienated the College of Cardinals, who voided his election and chose Clement VII to be pope. When Urban VI refused to yield the papacy, Clement ruled from Avignon. Christendom had two popes.

In 1409, a church council attempted to resolve the issue. The cardinals dismissed the existing popes and elected a third pope. For seven years, Christendom had three popes. With such chaos in leadership, there is little wonder why reformers like John Hus questioned church practices. In 1417, the Council of Constance (the same council that condemned Hus for heresy) deposed all three popes and elected Martin V, who returned the papacy to Rome.

3. Renaissance popes: The era of secular popes. After the Papal Schism came a succession of Renaissance popes whose conduct etched even greater tumult on the times. Let's consider a few of these men:

Sixtus IV (1471–1484) lived to make Rome a Renaissance city. He widened streets, built churches, cultivated the arts, organized choirs, and established the Vatican archives. When Sixtus wasn't promoting extravagant projects, he was promoting his family. Six of the thirty-four cardinals he appointed were his nephews, some of whom involved the pope in the scandalous murder of two of the Medicis, a ruling Renaissance family from Florence.

Alexander VI (1492–1503) was the ambitious, licentious, Spanish-born scoundrel, Rodrigo Borgia, who fathered several children, among them the ruthless Cesare and the infamous Lucrezia. (The Borgias were another powerful Renaissance family.) Alexander devoted his papacy to securing his children's advancement, largely through bribery, treachery, and assassinations. Girolamo Savonarola challenged Alexander's papacy and died as a result.

Leo X (1513–1521) was a Medici, a nepotist, and a double-tongued politician. He was sophisticated, widely traveled, and loved art, music, and the theater. When he became pope, Leo exclaimed, "Now that we have attained the papacy, let us enjoy it!"[4] Enjoy it, he did. Leo bankrupted the treasury. In his endeavor to refill the coffers, he pawned the palace furniture and relied heavily on the sale of indulgences, a fund-raising activity that placed him on a collision course with Martin Luther.[5]

4. Rigid practices: Inquisition and censorship. The call for reform resurrected repressive practices. Under the Renaissance popes, the Inquisition had been leniently pursued. But, in 1542, Pope Paul III (1534–1549), backed by Ignatius Loyola and Emperor Charles V, reinstated the Inquisition and added new rules. Inquisitors were to ignore rank, show no toleration, especially toward the Calvinists, and prosecute all clergy who did not preach against the Protestants. Inquisitors were also instructed to judge lesser offenses, like polygamy and fasting, which had nothing to do with heresy.

Under Paul IV (1555–1559), the "iron" pope, the Inquisition acquired, according to one cardinal, "such a reputation that from no other judgment seat on earth were more horrible and fearful sentences to be expected." The Inquisition was most severe in Italy and Spain and the least effective in England.

Paul IV also used censorship to control the content of printed material. He created the *imprimatur,* the official seal of approval that was stamped on all Catholic literature, and issued the *Index,* a list of condemned books and banned publishers. The sardonic Paolo Sarpi quipped that the *Index* was "the finest secret ever discovered for . . . making men idiotic." [6]

Self-Test

A. Famous foes of the Reformation Church Era. (Write the foe next to its appropriate statement.)

"Babylonian Captivity"   Renaissance popes   Papal Schism
Rigid practices

_____ Inquisition and censorship.

_____ The seventy-year period when popes were French and ruled from Avignon.

_____ Church leaders motivated by extravagance, nepotism, and politics.

_____ The period of multiple, rival popes.

B. Major foe of the Reformation Church Era. (Insert the name of the major foe on the blank.)

The major foe of the Reformation Church Era was _____
_____.

C. Wheel chart. (Place the name of the major foe on the wheel chart.)

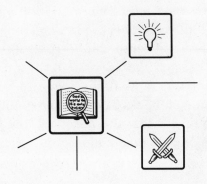

NINETEEN

KEY FIGURES: MEDIEVAL CHURCH PERIOD

O n Saturday, 5 May 1990, horse racing fans thrilled to the 116th running of the Kentucky Derby. Sportswriter Furman Bisher noted more than the win:

> A little lady older than this century arrived in the winner's circle at Churchill Downs on wheels Saturday afternoon to meet a friend of hers named Unbridled. She wore a polka-dot blouse and a little black pancake hat. He wore a blanket of roses.
>
> She made the trip in a wheelchair. He came on the four legs that had just carried him a mile and a quarter over a piece of Kentucky ground. It was a long time to wait, but at the age of 92, Mrs. Frances A. Genter had finally won a Kentucky Derby. [1]

Frances Genter and Unbridled certainly were an "odd couple" in the world of sports, but odd couples often make memorable history. This is especially true in the medieval church which had its share of disparate duos: Thomas Cranmer and Henry VIII, John Calvin and William Farel, and Martin Luther and Philip Melanchthon.

While our medieval study focuses only on the "big names" in church history, it is important to remember that, like Unbridled, those who come to the "winner's circle" seldom get there alone.

The Roman Church Era

I. Review:

Fill in the blanks to bring the wheel chart up to date.

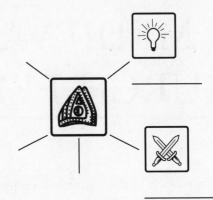

II. Key figure: Innocent III

Innocent III (1160–1216) was the most powerful pope in history. Innocent believed:

> The successor of Peter is the Vicar of Christ: he has been established as a mediator between God and man, below God but beyond man; less than God but more than man; who shall judge all and be judged by no one.[2]

Innocent reorganized the government of Rome, strengthened the papal states, influenced the election of the emperor, arranged a crusade, prevailed over two kings, and convened the pivotal (Innocent-dominated) Fourth Lateran Council (1215). Among its seventy rulings, the council endorsed the Franciscan Order, condemned the Magna Carta, and forced Jews and Muslims to wear special badges. The council also made transubstantiation a dogma of the church and required Christians to attend Easter Mass and to make an annual confession.

SUMMARY

The key figure of the Roman Church Era was _____.

III. Summary of other important figures:

1. Bernard of Clairvaux

2. Francis of Assisi

3. Medieval missionary monks

1. Bernard of Clairvaux: The first medieval mystic. Bernard (1090–1153) was the dominant figure of the twelfth century. He was the Abbot at Clairvaux, a Cistercian monastery, and exemplified what was best in monastic life. Bernard was dedicated, hardworking, and reform minded. He engendered trust and was the confidant of other abbots, kings, and popes. Bernard organized the Second Crusade and wrote the Rule for the Knights Templar, an order of crusading knights who guided pilgrims to the Holy Land.

Bernard was the first medieval mystic. His writings, *On Loving God* and the *Song of Songs,* reflected a life of prayer and self-denial. Bernard spent more than half of each day reading or studying Scripture, a habit which won him the respect of the Protestant Reformers. Martin Luther said that Bernard "was the best monk that ever lived, whom I admire beyond all the rest put together."[3]

2. Francis of Assisi: The founder of the Franciscans. Francis of Assisi (1181–1228) founded the Franciscans, an order of friars who lived out the vow of poverty. The Franciscans began their ministry as itinerant preachers in Italy. They worked or begged for their living, gave aid to the poor, and helped the sick. (Malaria and leprosy were rampant.) Friars were often beaten, robbed, and ridiculed, but their simple words and simple songs changed lives. Unlike traditional monastics, the Franciscans were laymen. Within a decade of their founding, there were more than five thousand Franciscan preachers, teachers, and missionaries.

Francis of Assisi is associated with the prayer which begins: "Lord, make me an instrument of thy peace. Where there is hatred, let me sow love . . ." While historians cannot positively accredit this prayer to Francis, similar thoughts are recorded in his writing, *Admonitions*:

> Where there is charity and wisdom, there is neither fear nor ignorance. Where there is patience and humility, there is neither anger nor vexation. Where there is poverty and joy, there is neither greed nor avarice. Where there is peace and meditation, there is neither anxiety nor doubt.[4]

3. Medieval missionary monks: The backbone of Christianity.
In spite of the rapid spread of Islam and the barbarian invasions, medieval missionary monks made thousands of converts. Five outstanding missionary monks were:

1. Augustine of Canterbury (d. 604?) evangelized the Angles and Saxons in England and harmonized the missionary efforts between the Roman and Celtic churches.

2. Boniface (680–754) was "the Apostle of the Germans" and worked closely with Pepin to reform the Frankish church. Boniface is remembered for dramatically cutting down an oak tree, a symbol of pagan worship, and using the wood to build a Christian church.

3. Cyril (826–869) and Methodius (c. 815–885), missionary brothers from the Eastern church, were the "Apostles to the Slavs." In 863, Cyril developed an alphabet for the as yet unwritten language of the Moravians, and the monks translated the Bible and other books into Slavic. Their work was later taken to the Bulgarians, the Serbians, and the Kievan

Russians. The alphabet used in Russia today is called cyrillic after the younger missionary.

4. Raymond Lull (c. 1232–1316) was a Franciscan who devoted his life to evangelizing Muslims. Lull made three missionary journeys to North Africa, opened a monastery for the study of Arabic on Majorca, campaigned for missionary training centers in Europe, and wrote books on Christian theology, many of which were written in Arabic.

Self-Test

A. Important figures of the Roman Church Era. (Write the figure next to the appropriate description.)

Bernard of Clairvaux   Innocent III   Francis of Assisi
Medieval missionary monks

_____ Founded the Franciscan order.

_____ Most powerful pope in history.

_____ Mystic monk associated with the Second Crusade.

_____ Converted the Angles, Saxons, Franks, Germans, Slavs, and Muslims.

B. Key figure of the Roman Church Era. (Insert the name of the key figure on the blank below.)

The key figure of the Roman Church Era was _____.

C. Wheel chart. (Place the name of the key figure on the wheel chart.)

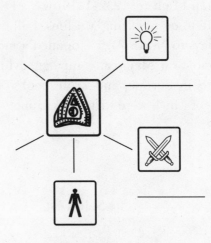

The Reformation Church Era

I. Review:

Fill in the blanks to bring the wheel chart up to date.

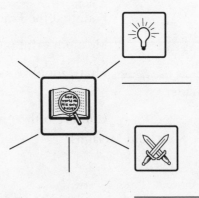

Note: The key figures of the Reformation Church Era represent the major Protestant traditions: Martin Luther/Lutheranism;

John Calvin/the Reformed tradition; Thomas Cranmer/the Anglican church; and Menno Simons/the Anabaptists.

II. Key figure: Martin Luther

Martin Luther (1483–1546) was the "Father of the Protestant Reformation." His spiritual struggles prompted him to study the Bible, where he found the verse that changed his life: "The just shall live by faith" (Romans 1:17, KJV). Luther remembered:

> Night and day I pondered until I saw the connection between the justice of God and the statement that "the just shall live by his faith." Then I grasped that the justice of God is that righteousness by which through grace and sheer mercy God justifies us through faith. Thereupon I felt myself to be reborn.[5]

Luther immediately recognized an inconsistency between Scripture and church teaching. In 1517, the routine practice of selling indulgences prompted him to post the Ninety-five Theses. This triggered a series of important meetings: the Leipzig Disputation (1519), the Diet of Worms (1521), the Marburg Colloquy (1529), and the Augsburg Confession (1530). Each meeting gave Luther the opportunity to refine his beliefs about the authority of Scripture, the roles of faith and grace, and the priesthood of believers. During these times Luther relied heavily on his friend, Philip Melanchthon, who wrote most of the Augsburg Confession, the Lutheran statement of faith.

Luther used the infant printing industry to spread his ideas. He wrote books, sermons, hymns, treatises, pamphlets, commentaries, and letters. He issued the German New Testament in 1521 and published the complete German Bible in 1534. Although excommunicated and branded a heretic, Luther lived to see many of his reforms adopted.

SUMMARY

The key figure of the Reformation Church Era was

_____ _____ .

III. Summary of other important figures:

1. John Calvin

2. Thomas Cranmer

3. Menno Simons

1. John Calvin: The focal figure of the Reformed tradition.
John Calvin (1509–1564) was a theologian and pastor who organized the Reformed tradition, that branch of Protestantism started
in Switzerland (c. 1520) by Ulrich Zwingli. The basic teachings of
Calvinism were set forth in the *Institutes of the Christian Religion*
(1536), Calvin's classic statement on Protestantism. At the heart of
Calvinism were five major points:

1. total depravity of man

2. unconditional election

3. limited atonement

4. irresistible grace

5. perseverance of the saints

This Reformed theology affected the development of the German and Dutch Reformed Churches along with the Baptist, Presbyterian, and the early Congregational Churches.

Based in Geneva, Calvin's ministry emphasized the sovereignty
of God and established the Christian commonwealth that Augustine had envisioned. Citizens affirmed a confession of faith and
were accountable to conduct themselves according to moral principles. While the commonwealth did not meet the approval of all
citizens, Geneva had its admirers. One refugee, Bernardino Ochino, described the city:

> Cursing and swearing, unchastity, sacrilege, adultery, and impure
> living, such as prevail in many places where I have lived, are here
> unknown. There are no pimps and harlots. The people do not
> know what rouge is, and they are all clad in seemly fashion.
> Games of chance are not customary. Benevolence is so great that

the poor need not beg. The people admonish one another in brotherly fashion, as Christ prescribes. Lawsuits are banished from the city. . . . On the other hand, there are no organs here, no voice of bells, no showy songs, no burning candles or lamps [in the churches], no relics, pictures, statues, canopies, or splendid robes, no farces or cold ceremonies. The churches are quite free from idolatry.[6]

2. Thomas Cranmer: The Reform leader of the Church of England. Thomas Cranmer (1489–1556) helped shape the Anglican church. Cranmer believed that the king, not the pope, had the right to govern the English church. Cranmer's views endeared him to Henry VIII (1491–1547), who started the English Reformation in 1530 by wresting power from the pope. In 1532, Henry appointed Cranmer the Archbishop of Canterbury, and for twenty-four turbulent years, Cranmer quietly reformed the practices of the Church of England.

Cranmer's most enduring contribution was *The Book of Common Prayer* (1549). Borrowing the best ideas from the Latin rituals, the Lutheran forms, and the Greek liturgies, he fashioned a single book written in English that contained the prescribed forms for public worship in the Anglican church. *The Book of Common Prayer* (along with the English Bible) became a stabilizing force in the development of the English language and influenced the prayer books of Lutherans, Methodists, Presbyterians, and Congregationalists.

3. Menno Simons: The focal figure of the Anabaptist movement. Menno Simons (1496–1561) was the chief spokesman for the Anabaptists, a radical offshoot of Zwingli's Swiss reform movement. Anabaptists were persecuted for their nontraditional beliefs: they disciplined their members, refused to wage war, and supported the separation of church and state. Unlike Catholics and Protestants, Anabaptists did not baptize babies; they practiced believer's baptism. Consequently, many were rebaptized as adults. *Anabaptist,* which meant "rebaptizer," was a term of scorn.

Because many Anabaptist leaders were martyred, the movement was near extinction in 1537, when Menno Simons infused new life. Simons settled in the Low Countries and took up itinerant preaching. He was labeled a heretic and tracked by bounty

hunters. Many of his followers were executed. But, as Simons established churches and propounded theology, he consolidated the
tenets and practices of the Dutch Anabaptists. From these seminal
beliefs sprang the Mennonites, Baptists, Brethren, and Amish.

Self-Test

**A. Important figures of the Reformation Church Era. (Write the
figure next to the appropriate description.)**

Menno Simons   John Calvin   Thomas Cranmer
Martin Luther

_____ Reform leader of the Church of England.

_____ Father of the Reformation.

_____ Itinerant Anabaptist theologian.

_____ Organized the Reformed tradition in
Geneva.

**B. Key figure of the Reformation Church Era. (Insert the name
of the key figure on the blank below.)**

The key figure of the Reformation Church Era was

_____   _____ .

**C. Wheel chart. (Place the name of the key figure on the wheel
chart.)**

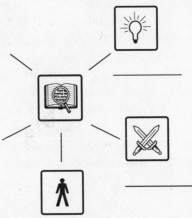

TWENTY

WRITERS/WRITINGS: MEDIEVAL CHURCH PERIOD

L iteracy was a barometer for the Middle Ages. In the rough and ready days of the Roman Church Era, reading and writing were "thumbs down" activities for most people. Serfs had no time for writing, and knights and lords were too busy planning their next war to read. Only clergymen were literate, and their language of choice was Latin. Consequently, many important writings from the Era, like the *Summa Theologiae* and *Pastoral Care*, were Latin texts written by clergymen for other clergy.

During the Reformation Church Era, the invention of printing and the manufacture of inexpensive paper created an interest in reading and writing. Literacy quickly became a status symbol, and writers began to articulate in vernacular languages. Because of the everwidening reading audience, many texts were written for laymen in vernacular languages; and some influential works, like *The Divine Comedy* and *The Canterbury Tales,* were written by laymen.

As you move through the writings of the Medieval Church Period, note how the subject matter increasingly appealed to the common man.

The Roman Church Era

I. Review:

Fill in the blanks to bring the wheel chart up to date.

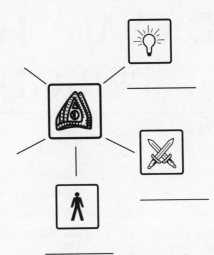

II. Key Writing: *Summa Theologiae*

Summa Theologiae was written by Thomas Aquinas (1225–1274), the greatest theologian of the Roman Church Era. Thomas lived during the age of chivalry, the Crusades, the Mongols, and Marco Polo, but Thomas was neither knight nor traveler; his adventures were mental. Thomas was a scholar, a Dominican who spent much of his life studying in Paris.

Thomas was attracted to Aristotle and abstracted from the philosopher's writings those ideas which were compatible with Christianity. Aquinas's observations became the basis for *Summa Theologiae* which focused on one issue: How may we know God?

Using a question/answer format—631 questions and 10,000 answers—Thomas studied the Scriptures, the early church writers, and the writings of the Greek, Muslim, and Jewish philosophers, made reasoned connections, and drew theological conclusions. Thomas intended "to set forth briefly and clearly the things which pertain to sacred doctrine . . . for the instruction of beginners." But Thomas thought on such a lofty level that few beginners could ever hope to wade through his twenty-one volume work.

Thomas Aquinas left an indelible mark on church history. His writings provided a reasoned interpretation of medieval Christian beliefs, and after the Reformation, they became the foundational teachings of the modern Roman Catholic church.

SUMMARY

The key writing of the Roman Church Era was the
_____ _____ .

III. Summary of Other Important Writings:

1. *Pastoral Care*

2. *Ecclesiastical History of the English People*

3. Urban II's Call for the First Crusade

1. *Pastoral Care*: The bishops' guide to leadership. *Pastoral Care* (c. 591) was a manual for bishops written by Pope Gregory the Great in which he urged pastors to balance their lives:

> Our Lord continued in prayer on the mountain, but wrought miracles in the cities; showing to pastors that while aspiring to the highest, they should mingle in sympathy with the necessities of the infirm.[1]

Yet, he lovingly warned them:

The leader should understand how often vices pass themselves off as virtues. Stinginess often excuses itself under the name of frugality while, on the other hand, extravagance hides itself under the name of generosity. Often inordinate laxity is mistaken for loving-kindness, while unbridled wrath is seen as the virtue of spiritual zeal.[2]

Pastoral Care was the standard text for church leadership during the Middle Ages and was translated into both Greek and Anglo-Saxon.

2. *Ecclesiastical History of the English People:* Early English life. The *Ecclesiastical History of the English People* was a carefully researched, five-volume account of England, from its earliest days to 731, that contained many anecdotes about early Christianity. The history was written by a monk, the Venerable Bede (c. 672–735), who lived in northern England. Bede spent most of his life at Jarrow, a monastery with an extraordinary library. Bede studied widely—the Bible, languages, chronology, poetry, music, biography, and science—and became the finest scholar in Europe. The years 600–800 were known as "the Age of Bede."

3. Urban II's Call for the First Crusade: The speech of the era. In November 1095, Pope Urban II inspired the first French Crusaders with this rousing address:

O race of Franks! race beloved and chosen by God! . . . From the confines of Jerusalem and from Constantinople a grievous report has gone forth that an accursed race, wholly alienated from God, has violently invaded the lands of these Christians, and has depopulated them by pillage and fire. They have led away a part of the captives into their own country, and a part they have killed by cruel tortures. . . . The kingdom of the Greeks [the Byzantine Empire] is now dismembered by them, and has been deprived of territory so vast in extent that it could not be traversed in two months' time.

On. whom, then, rests the labor of avenging these wrongs, and of recovering this territory, if not upon you. . . . Let the deeds of your ancestors encourage you—the glory and grandeur of Charlemagne and your other monarchs. Let the Holy Sepulcher of Our Lord and Saviour, now held by unclean nations arouse you, and the holy places that are now stained with pollution. . . . Let none of your possessions keep you back, nor anxiety for your family affairs. For this land which you now inhabit, shut in on all sides by the sea and the mountain peaks, is too narrow for your large population; it scarcely furnishes food enough for its cultivators. Hence it is that you murder and devour one another, that you wage wars, and that many among you perish in civil strife.

Let hatred, therefore, depart from among you; let your quarrels end. Enter upon the road to the Holy Sepulcher; wrest that land from a wicked race, and subject it to yourselves. . . . Undertake this journey eagerly for the remission of your sins, and be assured of the reward of imperishable glory in the Kingdom of Heaven.[3]

The crowd sanctified the plea by shouting "Dieu le veut!" ("God wills it!"), and medieval Europeans became crusaders for Christ.

Self-Test

A. Important writers of the Roman Church Era. (Match the writer to the correct statement.)

Thomas Aquinas   Gregory the Great   Urban II
Bede

_____ Wrote *Pastoral Care.*

_____ Issued the call for the First Crusade.

_____ Wrote *Summa Theologiae.*

_____ Wrote *Ecclesiastical History of the English People.*

B. Key writing of the Roman Church Era. (Insert the name of the key writing on the blank below.)

The key writing of the Roman Church Era was the

_____   _____.

C. Wheel chart. (Place the name of the key writing on the wheel chart.)

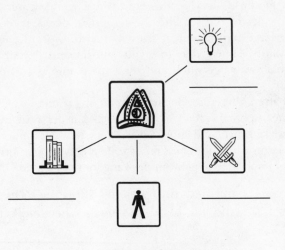

The Reformation Church Era

I. Review:

Fill in the blanks to bring the wheel chart up to date.

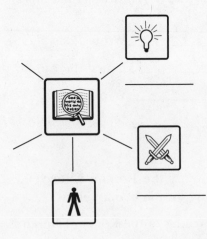

II. Key Writing: the English Bible

Developing the English Bible was a monumental undertaking. Two translators and two translations stand out.

William Tyndale (c. 1494–1536) vowed to a fellow clergyman to do something about biblical ignorance in England: "If God spare my life, ere many years pass I will cause a boy that driveth the plough shall know more of the Scriptures than thou dost." In exile, Tyndale published the first English New Testament in 1525. Copies were smuggled into England, where most were burned by the clergy. Tyndale was working on the Old Testament when he was executed as a heretic. He is called "the Father of the English Bible," and 90 percent of his work eventually found its way into the King James Bible.

Miles Coverdale (1488–1569) was an assistant to William Tyndale. Coverdale published the first complete English Bible, the Coverdale Bible, in 1535. Much of the elegant phrasing in modern English Bibles is due to Coverdale's influence.

The Great Bible (1539), edited by Miles Coverdale, was the first English Bible approved by Henry VIII. The Bible was called "great" because of its size; it was sixteen inches tall. The preface was written by Thomas Cranmer; consequently, it was often referred to as the Cranmer Bible. The Great Bible became the text for *The Book of Common Prayer.*

The Geneva Bible was an English Bible published in 1560 by Protestant exiles in Geneva. The translation was directed by John Knox and, perhaps, Miles Coverdale. The Geneva Bible was a vast improvement over the Great Bible. It was smaller, printed in readable roman type, and contained numbered verses, notes, maps, and prayers. The compact Geneva Bible encouraged private study and became so popular that it was printed for forty years after the appearance of the King James Bible. The Geneva Bible was the Bible of Shakespeare, John Bunyan, John Milton, Oliver Cromwell, the Puritans, and the Pilgrims.

SUMMARY

The key writing of the Reformation Church Era was the

_____ _____.

III. Summary of the Other Important Writings of the Era:

1. *The Divine Comedy*

2. *The Canterbury Tales*

3. *Imitation of Christ*

1. *The Divine Comedy:* **A poet's view of the afterlife.** Dante (1265–1321) wrote *The Divine Comedy,* a poem describing the poet's dream as he "traveled" through three realms of the afterlife: hell—a place of sin and despair, purgatory—a place for cleansing through faith, and Paradise—a place of redemption. Dante's companions on the journey were the poet Virgil, Beatrice (Dante's sweetheart), and Bernard of Clairvaux. Dante called the poem a comedy because the epic shifted from misery to happiness and because it was "written in a careless and humble style, in the vulgar tongue, which even housewives speak."[4] *The Divine Comedy* showcased scholastic thinking (although Thomas Aquinas would not have approved of the poet putting a pope in hell!) and told the story of salvation.

2. *The Canterbury Tales:* **Christian life in medieval England.** Geoffrey Chaucer (c. 1340–1400) wrote *The Canterbury Tales,* a comic poem about a fourteenth-century English pilgrimage that begins:

> When in April the sweet showers fall
> And pierce the drought of March to the root,
>   and all . . .
> Then people long to go on pilgrimages
> And palmers long to seek the stranger strands
> Of far-off saints, hallowed in sundry lands,
> And specially, from every shire's end
> In England, down to Canterbury they wend
> To seek the holy blissful martyr, quick
> To give his help to them when they were sick.

The Tales focus on twenty-nine pilgrims who are en route to the shrine of Thomas à Becket, the English saint who was murdered in Canterbury Cathedral in 1170. When Chaucer wrote *The Tales,* pilgrimages to Canterbury had been occurring for two hundred years.

Like Dante, Chaucer wrote in the vernacular—Middle English, the language of contemporary London. The prologue provided a wonderful glimpse of the men and women who peopled medieval Christianity, from the virtuous knight to the unscrupulous friar. Although Chaucer spoke openly against the abuses in the church, he was not a reformer. He was a writer who presented an English slice of Christian life.

3. *Imitation of Christ:* **The medieval call to spiritual renewal.** Thomas à Kempis (c. 1380–1471), a member of the Brethren of the Common Life, was the author of the *Imitation of Christ,* a popular medieval devotional and, next to the Bible, the most widely read book in the world. The *Imitation of Christ* persistently called its readers to spiritual renewal:

> What profit is it to us to live long, if in a long life we so little amend our life? Long life does not always bring us to amendment; often, it brings an increase of sin. Would to God that we might one day be truly converted in this world! Many count up their years of conversion, yet but little fruit of amendment or of any good example is seen in their manner of life. If it is fearful to die, perhaps it is more perilous to live long. Blessed are those who have the hour of death ever before their eyes, and who every day prepare themselves to die.[5]

Self-Test

A. Important writings of the Reformation Church Era. (Match the writing to the correct statement.)

Imitation of Christ   *The Divine Comedy*   The English Bible
The Canterbury Tales

_____ Dante's journey into the afterlife.

_____ Thomas à Kempis's widely read devotional.

_____ A trip to the shrine of Thomas a Becket.

_____ Associated with Tyndale and Coverdale.

B. Key writing of the Reformation Church Era. (Insert the name of the key writing on the blank below.)

The key writing of the Reformation Church Era was the

_____ _____.

C. Wheel chart. (Place the name of the key writing on the wheel chart.)

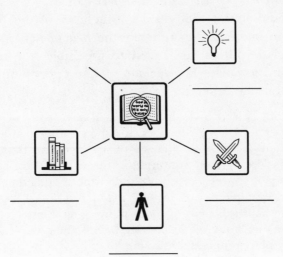

TWENTY-ONE

TRENDS: MEDIEVAL CHURCH PERIOD

A young dramatist, anxious for Carl Sandburg's opinion of his new play, asked the poet to attend the dress rehearsal. Sandburg slept through the performance. The playwright complained, saying that Sandburg had known how much he wanted his opinion. Sandburg listened, nodded, and quietly replied, "Sleep *is* an opinion."[1]

Sleep should not be a problem as we survey the medieval trends in building, art, worship, and music. There is simply too much going on to lapse into boredom. This is an exciting period, and one which should stimulate thought. The dominant trend in each era will appear as a boxed statement.

The Roman Church Era

I. Review:

Fill in the blanks to bring the wheel chart up to date.

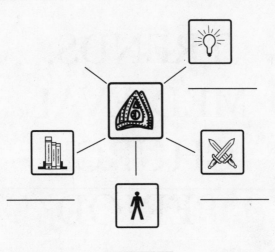

II. Dominant Trend: Church Building

During the eleventh century, church building boomed. France alone constructed 1,587 buildings. Ralph Glaber (985–1050), a monk/historian, describes the phenomenon:

> When the third year after the year 1000 approached, you could see churches being rebuilt almost everywhere, and above all in Italy and Gaul; although most of them had been very well constructed and did not really need this, keen rivalry moved each Christian community to have a more sumptuous church than that of its neighbours.[2]

Two architectural styles dominated the era: Romanesque and Gothic. Romanesque developed around 1000 and emphasized Roman and Byzantine details—arches and columns. Romanesque architecture found favor in the monasteries. The Gothic style developed about a century later and emphasized light. Selected characteristics of the two styles appear below:

Romanesque Architecture	Gothic Architecture
Round arches	Pointed arches
Vaulted ceilings	Unity of design
Few windows	Many windows
Thick columns	Stained glass
Heavy walls	Flying buttresses
Dark interiors	Light interiors
Horizontal emphasis	Vertical emphasis

The first Gothic building was the church of the Abbot of St. Denis, built outside Paris in 1144. The popularity of Gothic architecture precipitated a building craze known as the "cathedral crusade." Westminster Abbey, Notre Dame de Paris, and Cologne Cathedral were built during this time.

SUMMARY

The major trend of the Roman Church Era was

_____   _____.

III. Summary of Other Trends:

1. Worship

2. Music

3. Art

1. Worship: The seven sacraments. Around 1150, Peter Lombard formulated a list of seven sacraments which were approved by Thomas Aquinas and later embraced by the church. The seven sacraments included: Baptism, Penance, the Eucharist, Confirmation, Extreme Unction, Holy Orders, and Matrimony. Each sacrament involved a worship ceremony.

Baptism, the Eucharist, and Penance were especially important ceremonies. Baptism was a sign of salvation and church membership; all infants were baptized shortly after birth. The Eucharist was celebrated daily, but medieval Christians attached more importance to *seeing* the Eucharist than to receiving it. Many Christians only attended that portion of the Mass where the Eucharist was displayed.

Penance was a singular public admission of sin. Most people postponed the sacrament until they were old or dying. Between the seventh and tenth centuries, clergy assessed sins by consulting the Penitentials, books that contained lists of offenses with their corresponding "tariffs." Here are two penitentials from Bede:

> Anyone who kills a monk or a cleric shall . . . enter the service of God.
>
> The mother who kills the child she is carrying in her womb before the fortieth day following conception shall fast for one year; if it is after the fortieth day she shall fast three years.[3]

In 1215, a ruling issued by the Fourth Lateran Council required that all Christians confess their sins annually. Penance then became known as Confession.

2. Music: The beginnings of polyphony. Medieval music was vocal. Highly trained men and boys sang psalm texts, and the early songs, called Gregorian chants, were monophonic—all voices sang one melody—without measured rhythm or instrumental accompaniment.

Polyphony, harmonized or multipart music, began around 800 as choirs added vocal embellishments to basic chants. The clergy at Notre Dame in Paris developed two important polyphonic forms: the *organum* and the *motet*. The *organum* was a sacred composition in which a tenor sustained a base chant while another voice added rhythmic melody. The *motet* wove three to six voices around the base chant.

Musical notation trailed polyphony. During the tenth and eleventh centuries, notes were assigned letters of the alphabet, and the clef was introduced. A monk named Guido (death c. 1050) invented the musical staff and helped singers learn unfamiliar pieces more quickly by labeling the notes of the diatonic scale: *ut* (later changed to *do*), *re, mi, fa, sol, la, ti,* and *do.*

The earliest preserved popular music originated with the French troubadours in the twelfth century. Troubadours were poet/musicians who were called *minnesingers* in Germany and *trovatori* in Italy. Troubadours wrote about ladies and love.

By 1300, musical instruments abounded—bells, cymbals, timbrels, drums, lyre, harp, psaltery, lute, vielle (a short violin), viola, monochord, pipe, flute, hautboy (oboe), bagpipe, trumpet, organ, and horn—but they did not accompany the human voice.

3. Art: Gilding, sculpture, and stained glass. During the Dark Ages, Christian expressions of art were rare. One exception was the beautifully decorated manuscript, the *Lindisfarne Gospels,* produced by Irish monks around 700.

Public interest in art was heightened by the cathedrals, which, contrary to myth, were not built by hardworking volunteers. Cathedrals were the work of professional craftsmen—quarrymen, masons, carpenters, blacksmiths, and stone cutters—and exacting artists—sculptors, goldsmiths, glassmakers, and weavers—who left their masterpieces unsigned.

Romanesque churches were adorned with gilding, tapestries, and freestanding stone sculpture—a decorative feature that had not been used in Western churches for five hundred years. While in the Gothic churches, architectural elements, such as doors and windows, became occasions for art. At Chartres Cathedral, 175 stained-glass windows created a magnificent display of light and color. In addition, ten thousand figures adorned the church and two thousand statues filled its portals.

Self-Test

A. Trends of the Roman Church Era. (Identify the trend from its descriptive statement.)

Art   Music   Church building
Worship

_____ Gilding, sculpture, and stained glass.

_____ Seven sacraments.

_____ Gothic and Romanesque styles.

_____ The beginning of polyphony.

B. Dominant trend summary. (Fill in the box below with the correct answer.)

The dominant trend of the Roman Church Era was _____

_____ .

C. Wheel chart. (Place the dominant trend on the wheel chart.)

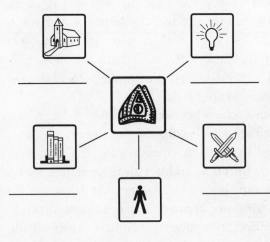

The Reformation Church Era

I. Review:

Fill in the blanks to bring the wheel chart up to date.

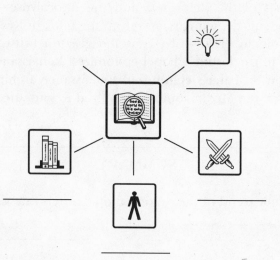

II. Dominant Trend: Church Art

Art dominated the Reformation Church Era. Two factors encouraged the trend: generous patrons and the "celebrity" artist. Let's look at some of the patrons and artists of the Reformation Church Era.

Patrons. Lorenzo de' Medici (1449–1492) was the greatest secular patron of medieval art. The Florentine banker/statesman collected objects of antiquity, for example, busts and statues, and paid promising artists, including Michelangelo, to emulate the artwork.

Pope Julius II (1503–1513) was the greatest papal patron of art. In 1508, he employed Raphael, the painter; Michelangelo, the sculptor; Bramante, the architect; and Fra Giovanni, the woodcarver.

Artists. Donato Bramante (1444–1514) was the great Italian architect hired to redesign St. Peter's in Rome.

Leonardo da Vinci (1452–1519) was the gifted Florentine artist, who is best remembered for the mural *The Last Supper* (commissioned for a monastery dining hall) and the portrait, the *Mona Lisa*.

Albrecht Durer (1471–1528) was a German artist known for his fine portraits of the Reformers and the Apocalypse—a series of fifteen woodcuts depicting scenes from the book of Revelation.

Michelangelo (1475–1564) was the greatest artist of the age. His ceiling in the Sistine Chapel epitomized Renaissance painting; his dome on St. Peter's epitomized Renaissance architecture; and his figures on the Medici tombs epitomized Renaissance sculpture.

SUMMARY

The major trend of the Reformation Church Era was
_____ _____.

III. Summary of Other Trends:

1. Church building

2. Ceremonies

3. Music

1. Church building: The Italian Renaissance style. Not everyone was happy with the Gothic style. "Cursed be the man who invented this wretched Gothic architecture!" cried Antonio Filarete in 1450. "Only a barbarous people could have brought it to Italy."[4]

Italian architects preferred the Renaissance style, with its colonnades, fluted columns, flowering capitals (the decorated uppermost part of columns), cornices, and domes. The finest example of the Italian Renaissance style was St. Peter's in Rome.

The original St. Peter's was built by Constantine in 330. In 1506, Pope Julius demolished the building and underwrote the construction of a new St. Peter's, completed in 1626. Bramante, Raphael, and Michelangelo were among the architects of the new church.

The new St. Peter's, with its dome and semicircular colonnades, was as spectacular as any Gothic cathedral. It measured 694 feet in length (roughly one-eighth of a mile), 451 feet in width, and reached an exterior height of 435 feet. The church, the largest in the world, showcased some of the world's great art treasures, including Michelangelo's *Pieta,* a sculpture of the crucified Christ with His grieving mother.

2. Ceremonies: Establishing Protestant worship. After the Reformation, worship ceremonies changed little for Catholics, but Protestants struggled to define their liturgies. Protestants modified or abolished the Mass and focused on preaching. The Bible became known as "God's Word," and there were two sacraments, Baptism and Communion. Holy days were abandoned. Prayer was no longer directed to Mary or the saints. Services were increasingly conducted in native languages, and congregational singing became a part of worship.

3. Music: Counterpoint and harmony. Music blossomed during the Reformation Church Era. Counterpoint came of age as the fugue wove four independent melodies into one harmonious sound. The madrigal, a contrapuntal song written in native languages, was born. Many madrigals were based on dance rhythms, which led musicians to emphasize chords (notes played simultaneously) and harmony (sound made by moving from chord to chord). The progression from counterpoint to harmony brought a demand for musical accompaniment.

Two popular instruments for accompaniment were the lute, the forerunner of the guitar, and the clavichord, the forerunner of the piano. The interest in instruments gave rise to the toccata, a solo composition for the organ that showcased the virtuosity of the performer. Listeners crammed into churches to hear organ concerts.

The music mania also prompted choral competitions, private chapels, and royal patronage. Kings selected their kapellmeisters (music directors) as carefully as their cooks. By 1510, sheet music was printed freely, and the socially astute read music *and* danced.

Dance forms included the vigorous morris (a Moorish dance), the stately pavane, the sprightly galliard, and the lively jig. Martin Luther enjoyed the "square dance, with friendly bows, embracings, and hearty swinging of the partners." [5]

Generally, clergymen gave the new music mixed reviews. Erasmus wrote:

> Modern church music is so constructed that the congregation cannot hear one distinct word. The choristers themselves do not understand what they are singing. . . . There was no [church] music in St. Paul's time. Words were then pronounced plainly. Words nowadays mean nothing. . . . Men . . . go to church to listen to more noises than were ever heard in Greek or Roman theaters. Money must be made to buy organs and train boys to squeal.[6]

Ulrich Zwingli, who played the lute, harp, violin, flute, and dulcimer, excluded all music from religious services. John Calvin banned polyphony and musical instruments but encouraged congregations to sing metrical psalms in unison. Only Martin Luther seemed in tune with the trend:

> When natural music is sharpened and polished by art, then one begins to see with amazement the great and perfect wisdom of God in His wonderful work of music, where one voice takes a simple part and around it sing three, four, or five other voices, leaping, springing round about, marvelously gracing the simple part. . . . He who does not find this an inexpressible miracle of the Lord is truly a clod. [7]

Self-Test

A. Trends of the Reformation Church Era. (Identify the trend from its descriptive statement.)

Church art   Music   Ceremonies
Church building

_____ The Italian Renaissance style.

_____ Associated with patronage and "celebrity" artists.

_____ Harmony comes of age.

_____ Establishing Protestant worship.

B. Dominant trend summary. (Fill in the box below with the correct answer.)

The dominant trend of the Reformation Church Era was

_____   _____.

C. Wheel chart. (Place the dominant trend on the wheel chart.)

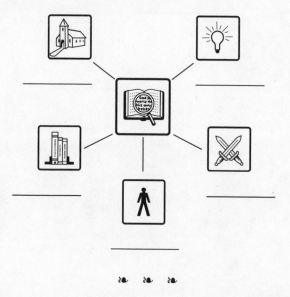

This chapter concludes our study of the Medieval Church Period. Tomorrow, we will look at the more familiar Modern Church Period.

THE MODERN
CHURCH PERIOD

TWENTY-TWO

GEOGRAPHY: MODERN CHURCH PERIOD

T he geography of the Modern Church Period covers the globe. Did you know that:

- In 1750, Philadelphia was the largest city in North America with a population of nearly twenty thousand.
- *Defenestration,* which means "throwing something out of the window," was a fashionable way of dethroning royalty in Europe.
- In 1792, freed slaves from America colonized the new nation, Sierra Leone, in West Africa.
- The Mormons, Seventh Day Adventists, Jehovah's Witnesses, and Christian Scientists had their beginnings in nineteenth-century America.
- In 1820, it took five months to sail from New England to Hawaii.
- The worst famine in modern history occurred in China from 1876 to 1879 and claimed the lives of thirteen million people.
- Steerage rates for immigrants to the United States were cut to ten dollars in 1904.

- Currently, the four major areas of population concentration in the world are: eastern North America, western Europe, South Central Asia (India and Bangladesh), and the Far East (Japan and eastern China).
- Mandarin Chinese is the most widely spoken language in the world today.

To broaden our understanding of the modern phase of Church history, let's look at some of the important places by era.

The Denominational Church Era

As you read each description, write the name of the place beside its corresponding number/letter on Map I (see page 212).

Countries

- *France* (I). During the Denominational Church Era, France was preoccupied with war: civil war between the Huguenots (French Protestants) and the Catholics, war with Spain, war with the Netherlands, and war with the British. Paris, the hub of French activity, was the city of the famous Bourbon dynasty—King Louis XIII, XIV, XV, and XVI—Cardinal Richelieu, Marie Antoinette, Moliere, and Voltaire.
- *England* (II). England was the focal area of the Denominational Church Era. It was also the mother country of the American colonies, the birthplace of several influential denominations, and the home of the great religious writers: John Foxe, John Milton, and John Bunyan. During this era, England experienced many internal stresses—Civil War, the Commonwealth, the Protectorate, and the return to a constitutional monarchy; yet, it developed into a world power.
- *The Holy Roman Empire* (III). The Holy Roman Empire was the site of one of the bloodiest religious wars, the Thirty Years' War (1616–1648).
- *Spain* (IV). Spain, once a great international colonial power, began to disintegrate during the Denominational Church Era.

Spain's decline was hastened by autocratic leadership, the destruction of its Armada in 1588, and the Thirty Years' War.

- *The Netherlands* (V). The Netherlands, part of the Low Countries, borders the North Sea. Much of the area is at or below sea level and is protected by an elaborate system of canals and dikes. During this era, the Netherlands derived immense wealth from manufacturing and trade. In 1557, it was under the control of Philip, the Spanish Hapsburg king.

Cities

- *Trent* (1). Trent is a small town located in the heart of the Alps in modern Italy. In 1546, the town hosted the Council of Trent, the pivotal church council that responded to the Protestant call for reform.

- *Herrnhut* (2). Herrnhut was a community of Christian refugees located in Saxony on the estate of Count Nikolaus von Zinzendorf. Herrnhut became the headquarters of the influential Moravian Brethren.

Missions

- *The American colonies* (A). From their inception, the American colonies were tied to Christianity. During the early eighteenth century, large numbers of Pietist (evangelical) immigrants and missionaries came to the colonies and supported the revivals called the Great Awakening (1725–1760). These revivals refocused the commitment of the colonists and indirectly inspired the American Revolution.

SUMMARY

The focal area of the Denominational Church Era was
_____.

The Global Church Era

As we examine the Global Church Era, we will update information about some of the countries we have already studied and learn

Map I

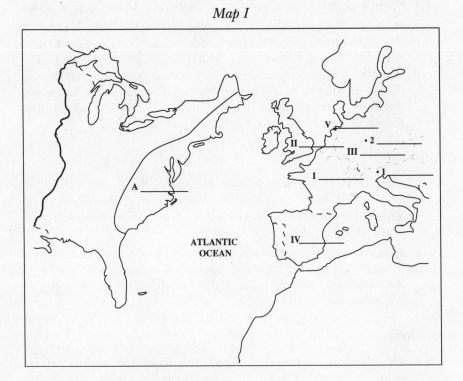

new facts about other places. As you read each description, write the name of the place besides its number/letter on Map II (see page 213).

Countries

- *France* (I). The modern nation of France emerged after the French Revolution. The revolutionary ideals fostered in France were spread throughout Europe as Napoleon attempted to build an empire.

- *England* (II). Under Queen Victoria (1837–1901), England became one of the focal nations of the world.

- *Germany* (III). In 1804, Napoleon divided the Holy Roman Empire. As a result, a nucleus of central European territories with strong cultural ties began to develop into the modern nation of Germany.

Map II

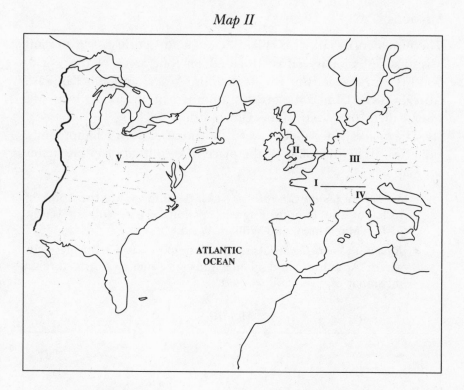

- **Italy** (IV). Italy was established as a modern nation in 1871. Its unification impacted Catholic Christianity in two significant ways: (1) the land holdings of the church were reduced to the Vatican, Lateran, and Castel Gandolfo; and (2) the pope was no longer recognized as a temporal ruler. Between 1870 and 1929, relations between the Italian government and the papacy were so strained that the papacy refused to acknowledge the Italian civil authority and no pope set foot outside the Vatican.

- **The United States** (V). By the beginning of the Global Church Era, the United States was an independent nation. The Second Great Awakening (1795–1835) infused the young country with a moral purpose and religious vigor that helped it survive the severe internal stresses of the nineteenth century. During the twentieth century, the United States became a world power, a recognized leader in missions, and one of the focal areas of the world.

Missions

The nineteenth century is called "The Great Century of Protestant Missions." Missionary efforts focused on four areas of the world: South Central Asia, the Pacific Islands, Africa, and the Far East. Africa, which claimed the greatest numbers of missionary lives, was often called "the White Man's Graveyard."

The places listed below were the home bases of famous missionaries. Write the name of the place next to its appropriate letter on Map III.

- *Serampore (South Central Asia)* (A). Serampore was the home in India of the famous English missionary trio William Carey, Joshua Marshman, and William Ward.

- *Rangoon (South Central Asia)* (B). Rangoon was the Burmese city where Adoniram and Nancy Judson, America's first foreign missionaries, lived and worked.

Map III

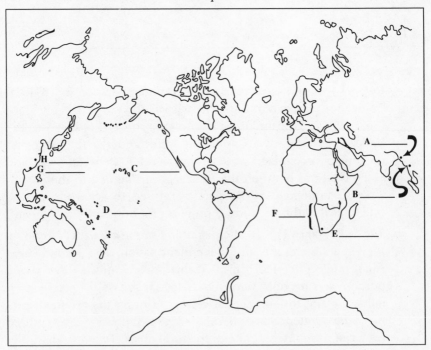

- **The Hawaiian Islands (the Pacific Islands)** (C). The Hawaiian Islands (formerly called the Sandwich Islands) were the mission field of Hiram Bingham, a native New Englander, who built the first Christian church in Honolulu in 1821.

- **Polynesia (the Pacific Islands)** (D). Tahiti and the surrounding Polynesian islands were the focus of the English missionary, John Williams, who was also called the "Apostle of the South Seas."

- **Capetown (Africa)** (E). Capetown was the port of entry into Africa for the Scottish missionary, Robert Moffat, and his wife, Mary, who established a Christian farm compound, Kuruman, six hundred miles northeast of the city.

- **South Africa** (F). The internationally acclaimed missionary, David Livingstone, explored the bush area of South Africa.

- **Canton (the Far East)** (G). Canton served as the "language laboratory" for Robert Morrison, the missionary/linguist who compiled an English-Chinese dictionary and translated the Bible into Chinese.

- **Shanghai (the Far East)** (H). Shanghai was the home base of Hudson Taylor and his innovative mission society, the China Inland Mission.

SUMMARY

The focal areas of the Global Church Era were_____ and the _____ _____ .

Self-Test

A. Match the names of the important places of the Denominational Church Era with their descriptions.

England   The Holy Roman Empire   Herrnhut
American Colonies

_____ Location of revivals called the Great Awakening.

_____ Focal area of the Denominational Church Era.

_____ Headquarters of the Moravian Brethren.

_____ Site of the Thirty Years' War.

B. Match the names of the important places of the Global Church Era with their descriptions.

England and the United States   Africa   Shanghai
"The Great Century of Protestant Missions,"

_____ Called the "White man's graveyart

_____ The nineteenth century.

_____ Focal areas of the Global Church Era.

_____ Home base of the missionary, Hudson Taylor.

TWENTY-THREE

STORY LINE: DENOMINATIONAL CHURCH ERA

T he courier delivered his report to the old Chinese general: "Sixteen thousand Chinese dead. Two hundred sixty-four Japanese killed." The general nodded.

The next day the messenger returned: "Eleven thousand Chinese dead; one hundred ninety-four Japanese killed." The general nodded.

The third day, the messenger reported: "Twenty-one thousand Chinese dead; three hundred and twelve Japanese killed."

The general smiled and rubbed his hands together. "Ah," he said slowly, "pretty soon, no more Japanese."[1]

By the sixteenth century, Christianity, like the old general, had lost sight of its mandate. Christians had become militant churchmen who believed that all truth was theirs and error demanded punishment. For one hundred years (1550–1650), persecution, Inquisition, and war rained down on Europe. In Holland, Calvinists murdered Catholics. In France, Jesuits endorsed regicide (killing the king). In Germany, Lutherans imprisoned Anabaptists. In England, Anglicans condemned Methodists, and the Quakers heckled everyone.

The Denominational Church Era, one of the most chaotic periods of Church history, is important because it set the stage for the modern era. Step lively through this fitful time.

The Denominational Church Era

I. Review:

Fill in the Story of Church History

Period	Era	Date	Epoch	Pivotal Church Figure	Story Line
Ancient Church					Bishops _____ the churches as the congregations grew, developed distinct _____, and suffered _____.
					Theologians _____ the church, upheld its _____, and continued its _____.
Medieval Church					Monks _____ the barbarians, transmitted and _____ culture and _____ leadership.
					Reformers _____ the teachings and _____ of the church and called for _____.
Modern Church					

II. Story Line Summary:

Churchmen *fought* over dogma, *settled* new colonies, and contended with Enlightened *thinking*.

SUMMARY

Churchmen_____ over dogma, _____ new colonies, and contended with Enlightened _____.

III. Expansion:

Four forces that dominated the Denominational Church Era were:

1. Council of Trent

2. Wars of religion

3. United States colonization

4. The Enlightenment

1. Council of Trent: Modern Catholicism is established. Councils had traditionally settled church disputes. However, more than twenty-five years lapsed after Luther posted his Theses before Pope Paul III convened the Council of Trent (1545–1563). The council, dominated by southern Europeans, met in three stages over an eighteen-year period. Only thirty-four of the five hundred delegates attended the first meeting, while less than half (237 delegates) approved the final decisions. Among its decisions, the council:

- defined modern Catholic beliefs and rituals. The council embraced the theology of Thomas Aquinas, made church tradition of equal authority with Scripture, upheld the dogmas of transubstantiation and justification by faith *and* works, reaffirmed the practice of clerical celibacy and indulgences, and retained Latin as the official language of the church. By negating the Protestant issues, the Council of Trent ended all hope of Protestant-Catholic reconciliation.

- suggested reforms. Delegates recommended an official training program for the clergy which led to the founding of seminaries. Abusive practices, such as clerical concubinage, were condemned.

- ordered the revision of the Latin Vulgate and the inclusion of the Apocrypha.

- reaffirmed the authority of the pope. The implementation of many conciliar decisions was left to the discretion of the pope.

2. Wars of religion: Doctrine, politics, and nationalism. The Protestant Reformation upset the spiritual and the political balance of Europe. For one hundred years (1550–1650), wars were waged as religious issues sanctified national struggles for power. Here are some of the countries involved in the religious wars:

The Netherlands. Philip II of Spain (1556–1598), the son of Charles V, was a dominant leader in the religious wars. Philip was a devout Catholic who was determined to wipe out Protestantism. In 1557, Philip levied harsh taxes against the Netherlands, reinstated the Inquisition, and resurrected his father's edicts against heretics (under Charles, fifty thousand Protestants had been executed). Philip's heavy-handed measures sparked the Dutch war (1560–1618) for independence from Spain.

France. Catholic France had long used persecution to control Protestant "heresy." By 1560, the Huguenots (French Protestants) had gained enough power to trigger a civil war over their increased demands for recognition. Hostilities increased in 1572 when Catholics murdered two thousand Protestants gathered in Paris for a royal wedding. The incident, called the St. Bartholomew's Day Massacre, triggered riots in the countryside, where another ten thousand Huguenots were slain. The Edict of Nantes, issued in 1598, finally ended the persecution of the French Huguenots.

England. In 1558, under Queen Elizabeth, the Church of England officially became Protestant. Catholic sympathizers, however, still dreamed of deposing the queen and returning England to the papacy. Philip II joined the effort when he unsuccessfully launched his Spanish Armada against Britain in 1588.

Religious conflicts among the Protestants, Parliament, and the monarchy continued during the seventeenth century and led to the overthrow of the Anglican church (1642), Civil War (1642–1649), the establishment of the Commonwealth* (1649–1653) and the Protectorate† (1653–1660), and eventually, the restoration of the monarchy (1660).

The Holy Roman Empire. The Thirty Years' War (1616–1648), the most well known religious conflict, began in the German states over a dispute between Calvinists and Catholics. By the time the war ended, Germany, Denmark, France, Austria, Spain, and Sweden were involved; and Protestants and Catholics had fought both with and against each other. Interestingly, the fighting was more over land and power than over theology and ritual. The complicated settlement, called the Peace of Westphalia (1643–1648), took more than four years to negotiate. The settlement returned Germany to the religious status of 1529, granted rulers the right to choose the faith of their country, and prohibited the pope from interfering in the religious matters of Germany.

3. United States colonization: A refuge for religious dissenters.
Concentrated British emigration to the American colonies started under James I (1603–1625) and continued under his son, Charles I (1625–1649). While the colonies were primarily business ventures, colonists were also lured to America by the opportunity for religious freedom. Between 1620 and 1642, more than twenty-five thousand Puritans emigrated to New England.

All of the original thirteen colonies had Protestant beginnings except Maryland, which was a Catholic settlement. The southern

---

* The English Commonwealth was a republic run by a Puritan Parliament and supported by the army of Oliver Cromwell. There was no king; Charles I had been beheaded early in 1649.

† The Protectorate was rule by Cromwell, who functioned as a dictator. He was called "Lord Protector" but had all the powers of a king.

colonies—Virginia, the Carolinas, and Georgia—were Anglican. Connecticut, Massachusetts, and New Hampshire were Congregational (a blending of Puritan and Separatist beliefs). New Jersey and New York were Reformed. Rhode Island was settled by Baptists, Pennsylvania by Quakers, and Delaware by the Swedish Lutherans. As the colonies prospered, other religious groups came. During the eighteenth century, seventy thousand German Pietists settled the northern colonies.

At first, religious zeal permeated the colonies, but then prosperity set in, enthusiasm waned, and by 1680 (forty years before the Great Awakening), American ministers were calling for revival.

4. The Enlightenment: The Age of Reason. The Enlightenment, or the Age of Reason, was a widespread intellectual revolution that occurred between 1648–1789 as man began to evaluate God and the world on the basis of reason and scientific principles rather than scriptural revelation.

The philosophers and writers of the Enlightenment promoted human welfare, independent thinking, science, religious toleration, and the principles of democratic government. These intellectuals believed that man was intrinsically good but that he had been corrupted by society.

The Enlightened thinkers held divergent opinions about Christianity. Some tried to reconcile reason and faith, giving each a "sphere of influence." Others dismissed the Scriptures altogether, labeling them "superstition" or "myth." Most Enlightened thinkers were not daring enough to publicly espouse atheism. They cloaked God in the concept of a "Supreme Being."

Among the leading figures of the Enlightenment were David Hume (1711–1776) in Scotland, John Locke (1632–1704) and Edward Gibbon (1737–1794) in England, Immanuel Kant (1724–1804) in Germany, Thomas Jefferson (1743–1826) in America, and Jean Jacques Rousseau (1712–1778) and Voltaire (1694–1778) in France. Paris was the hub of Enlightenment thinking.

Self-Test

To check your answers, review the previous pages.

A. Four forces that dominated the Denominational Church Era. (Match each force to its descriptive statement.)

Council of Trent   U.S. Colonization   Wars of Religion
The Enlightenment

_____ One hundred years of conflict.

_____ A haven for religious dissenters.

_____ The Age of Reason.

_____ Established modern Catholicism.

B. Story Line Summary. (Fill in the blanks from memory.)

Churchmen_____ over dogma, _____ new
colonies, and contended with Enlightened _____.

C. Arc of Church History. (Fill in the names of the Eras.)

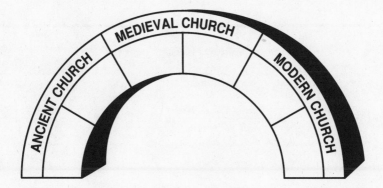

D. Story of Church History. (Complete the Story of Church History.)

Period	Era	Date	Epoch	Pivotal Church Figure	Story Line
Ancient Church					Bishops _____ the churches as the congregations grew, developed distinct _____ , and suffered_____ .
					Theologians _____ the church, upheld its _____, and continued its _____.
Medieval Church					Monks _____ the barbarians, transmitted and _____ culture, and _____ leadership.
					Reformers _____ the teachings and _____ of the church and called for _____.
Modern Church					Churchmen _____ over dogma, _____ new colonies, and contended with Enlightened _____.

TWENTY-FOUR

STORY LINE: GLOBAL CHURCH ERA

T he label read: manufactured in New Jersey. The phrase conjured images of busy factories and mass production.

Although the word *manufacture* seems modern, the term originally was used in medieval cottage industries and literally meant "made by hand." This abrupt shift in meaning typifies the changes that occurred during the Global Church Era. New words, new phrases—*sweat shop, laissez-faire, inflation,* and *mass evangelist*—identified new concepts.

To understand more about the dynamic times of the Global Church Era, let's look at three revolutions and the systems of thought that inspired them.

The Global Church Era

I. Review:

Fill in the blanks for the Story of Church History.

Period	Era	Date	Epoch	Pivotal Church Figure	Story Line
Ancient Church					Bishops _____ the churches as the congregations grew, developed distinct _____ , and suffered_____ .
					Theologians _____ the church, upheld its _____, and continued its _____.
Medieval Church					Monks _____ the barbarians, transmitted and _____ culture, and _____ leadership.
					Reformers _____ the teachings and _____ of the church and called for _____.
Modern Church					Churchmen _____ over dogma, _____ new colonies, and contended with Enlightened _____.

II. Story Line Summary:

Strategists faced a shifting *world order,* coped with social and political *changes,* and found new ways to share their Christian faith at home and *abroad.*

SUMMARY

Strategists faced a shifting _____ _____, coped with social and political _____, and found new ways to share their Christian faith at home and _____.

III. Expansion:

Four forces that dominated the Global Church Era were:

1. French Revolution

2. Industrial Revolution

3. Artistic Revolution

4. Ideologies

1. The French Revolution: Violent political change. The Global Church Era started as the epochal French Revolution abolished the monarchy (a thousand-year tradition called "the divine right of kings"), established a republic (1795), and promoted revolutionary ideals. It was one thing for the rag-tag British colonies in America to declare their independence, but quite another for a staid European nation to become unstable. The violence caused shock waves throughout Western civilization.

The French Revolution began in Paris in 1789, after Louis XVI reconvened the French Parliament ("adjourned" since 1614) to deliberate the national debt. The peasant's division of the parliament declared itself the legitimate legislative arm of France. When the king did not agree, a mob stormed the Bastille, released the prisoners, and destroyed the building. The commemoration of that event on 14 July 1789 is called Bastille Day and is the most significant national holiday in France.

A constitutional monarchy was instituted immediately, but the king and his queen, Marie Antoinette, were reluctant participants and were guillotined in 1793. Control of the government then passed to Robespierre, who ruled with a "reign of terror." After Robespierre, a ruling council, the Directory, was created. The ineptitude of this body set the stage for the rise of Napoleon in 1799 which, in turn, signaled the end of the French Revolution.

2. Industrial Revolution: Economic growth and social upheaval. The Industrial Revolution was a period of rapid economic growth and violent social upheaval. The revolution began in England around 1750, traveled quickly to the United States, but meandered more slowly through war-torn Europe. The Industrial Revolution was triggered by inventions—such as the steam engine, the spinning jenny, and the power loom—which allowed manufacturers to produce high quality goods while lowering production costs.

Industrialization forced employees into loathsome factory settings. Buildings were noisy. Hours were long. Tasks were monotonous. Wages were low. Women and children, who made up the bulk of the work force, were exploited and abused. Consider this official testimony given by Elizabeth Bentley in England around 1815:

> *What age are you?*
> Twenty-three . . .
>
> *What time did you begin work at the factory?*
> When I was six years old . . .
>
> *What kind of mill is it?*
> Flax mill.
>
> *What was your business in that mill?*
> I was a little doffer [explained below].
>
> *What were your hours of labour in the mill?*
> From five in the morning till nine at night, when they were thronged [busy] . . .
>
> *Explain what you had to do.*
> When the frames are full, they have to stop the frames, and take the flyers off, and take the full bobbins off, and carry them to the roller, and then put empty ones on, and set the frame going again.
>
> *Does that keep you constantly on your feet?*
> Yes, there are so many frames, and they run so quick.
>
> *Your labour is very excessive?*
> Yes, you have not time for anything.

Suppose you flagged a little, or were late, what would they do?
Strap us.

And they are in the habit of strapping those who are last in doffing?
Yes.

Constantly?
Yes.

Girls as well as boys?
Yes.

Have you ever been strapped?
Yes . . .

Is the strap used so as to hurt you excessively?
Yes it is . . . I have seen the overlooker go to the top end of the room, where the little girls hug the can to the backminders; he has taken a strap, and a whistle in his mouth, and sometimes he has got a chain and chained them, and strapped them all down the room.

What was his reason for that?
He was very angry . . .

You are considerably deformed in person as a consequence of this labour?
Yes I am.

And what time did it come on?
I was about thirteen years old when it began coming, and it has got worse since; it is five years since my mother died, and my mother was never able to get me a good pair of stays to hold me up, and when my mother died I had to do for myself, and got me a pair.

Were you perfectly straight and healthy before you worked at a mill?
Yes, I was as straight a little girl as ever went up and down town . . .

Did your deformity come upon you with much pain and weariness?
Yes, I cannot express the pain all the time it was coming.

Do you know of anybody that has been similarly injured in their health?
Yes, in their health, but not many deformed as I am.

It is very common to have weak ankles and crooked knees?
Yes, very common indeed.

This is brought on by stopping the spindle?
Yes.

Where are you now?
In the poorhouse.

State what you think as to the circumstances in which you have been placed during all this time of labour, and what you have considered about it as to the hardship and cruelty of it.
The witness was too much affected to answer the question.[1]

3. Artistic Revolution: The romantic movement. Romanticism was an eighteenth-century artistic/literary/philosophic movement. Romanticism reacted against reason. The romantic thinker was emotional, sensuous, and imaginative; he created worlds filled with warmth, color, and passion, and basked in extremes—from unrestrained joy to abysmal melancholy. The romantic appreciated the past (especially the Middle Ages), anticipated the future, and was fascinated by death. Romantics enjoyed poetry and autobiography; they focused on nature and humanitarianism. Romantics created a faith—not orthodox Christianity, but a personal religion sprinkled with naturalism, materialism, and pantheism. Church strategists, like John Wesley, capitalized on the humanitarian interest with projects—visiting poorhouses and prisons, for example—that motivated Christians with biblical injunctions.

Some of the famous romantics of the era were the painter Joseph Turner; the composers, Robert Schumann, Felix Mendelssohn, Johannes Brahms, and Frederic Chopin; and the writers, Johann Goethe, Victor Hugo, William Wordsworth, Samuel Taylor Coleridge, William Blake, Lord Byron, John Keats, and Percy Bysshe Shelley.

4. Ideologies: New systems of political thought. During the Global Church Era, society increasingly focused on power and the accumulation of wealth. The era gave rise to new ideologies, systems of political, economic, and social thought. These ideologies fostered religious-like adherence: they made demands, had a recognized body of writings, and were led by strong personalities. To

varying degrees, these ideologies undermined the tenets and practices of Christianity. Here in brief are five of these ideologies:

1. *Capitalism* was the economic/political system which featured
   both private and corporate ownership and open competition in a free market.

2. *Totalitarianism* was the complete domination of a country by its
   government. Totalitarian governments, which were run by a
   single political party and led by strong leaders or small, elite
   groups, controlled all social, political, and economic activities.

3. *Fascism* was a right-wing (conservative, reactionary) form of
   totalitarianism. It was a system of government dominated by
   a powerful dictator (for example, Mussolini, Hitler, or
   Franco) who wore a military uniform, inspired followers by
   public parades, and appealed to nationalistic fervor. Hatred
   for minority groups characterized fascism.

4. *Communism* was a left-wing (liberal, radical) form of totalitarianism. Its goal was a classless society where all means of
   production would be collectively owned and controlled by
   the government. Two leading spokesmen for communism
   were Karl Marx and Friedrich Engels. They wrote *The Communist Manifesto* (1848), the document which proclaimed
   the principles of communism and concluded: "Workers of
   the world, unite."

5. *Socialism* was the economic/political system in which government, not private enterprise, controlled the production and
   distribution of goods; and cooperation, not competition,
   guided economic activity. While some socialists tolerated
   capitalism, others abolished private enterprise altogether.
   Karl Marx viewed socialism as a stage between capitalism
   and communism.

So pervasive were these new systems of thought that in 1864,
Pope Pius IX (1846–1878) condemned the ideologies in his *Sylla-
bus of Errors* and convened a church council, Vatican I, to reestab-

lish his authority. Among evangelicals, the ideologies forced all strategists—missionaries, revivalists, evangelists, and linguists—to find new ways to share their faith.

Self-Test

A. Four forces that dominated the Global Church Era. (Match each force with its correct description.)

French Revolution   Artistic Revolution   Industrial Revolution
Ideologies

_____ Changed production techniques and working conditions.

_____ Systems of thought about economics, politics, and society.

_____ Abolished the thousand-year rule of kings.

_____ Reacted against reason; stressed emotions and the imagination.

B. Story Line Summary. (Fill in the blanks from memory.)

Strategists faced a shifting _____ _____, coped with social and political _____, and found new ways to share their Christian faith at home and _____.

C. Arc of Church History. (Fill in the the names of the eras.)

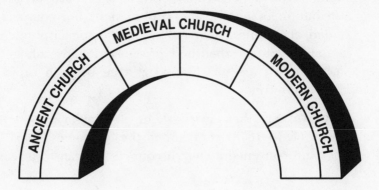

D. Story of Church History. (Complete the Story of Church History.)

Period	Era	Date	Epoch	Pivotal Church Figure	Story Line
Ancient Church					Bishops _____ the churches as the congregations grew, developed distinct _____, and suffered _____.
					Theologians _____ the church, upheld its _____, and continued its _____ .
Medieval Church					Monks _____ the barbarians, transmitted and _____ culture, and _____ leadership.
					Reformers _____ the teachings and _____ of the church and called for _____.
Modern Church					Churchmen _____ over dogma, _____ new colonies, and contended with Enlightened _____.
					Strategists faced a shifting _____ _____ coped with social and political_____ , and found new ways to share their Christian faith at home and _____ .

TWENTY-FIVE

HEADLINES: MODERN CHURCH PERIOD

W ho and what shaped the headlines of modern history?
Certainly, strong personalities: Elizabeth I, Cromwell,
Captain Cook, Napoleon, Lincoln, Queen Victoria, Wood-
row Wilson, Charles Lindbergh, Adolf Hitler, Winston Churchill,
John F. Kennedy, and in recent days, Saddam Hussein.

Wars cornered a share of the attention: the Thirty Years' War,
the English Civil War, the American Revolution, the French Revolution, the Napoleonic Wars, the American Civil War, the Spanish-
American War, World War I, World War II, the Korean War, the
Vietnam War, and the Persian Gulf War.

Lest we forget, modern history has chronicled its share of disasters: the Great Fire of London, the Irish potato famine, the Chicago fire, the sinking of the *Titanic,* the influenza epidemic of
1918, the Alaskan earthquake, and the East African famine.

But not all news was bad news. Modern exploration continued on
a grand scale. Drake sailed the world. Livingstone charted Africa.
Hudson penetrated Canada. America was settled. Peary reached the

North Pole, and Amundsen, the South Pole. Armstrong and Aldrin walked on the moon.

These people and events affected the world in much the same way that the Roman baths and the medieval Mongols influenced earlier times. To gain more insight into the picturesque diversity of modern incidents, let's examine four historical events, all eye-witness accounts. The articles describe (in order of appearance) a war, a personality, a disaster, and a triumph of exploration. A brief note at the beginning of each selection identifies the author(s) and provides the historical context.

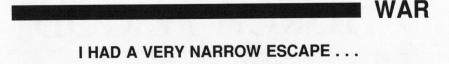

WAR

I HAD A VERY NARROW ESCAPE . . .

This account of a sea battle was written by James Anthony Gardner, a twelve-year-old midshipman. The military engagement took place on 20 October 1782.

The action continued from six P.M. until three-quarters past ten; the van and rear chiefly engaged; the centre had little to do. . . . We had four killed and sixteen wounded; among the former Mr. Robert Sturges, midshipman doing duty as mate, a gentleman highly respected and lamented by every officer and man on board. . . . He was as brave a fellow as ever lived, and when his thigh was nearly shot off by the hip, he cheered the men when dying. It was a spent shot that killed him and weighed twenty-eight pounds; and what was remarkable, it took off at the same time the leg of a pig in the sty under the forecastle [the upper deck of a ship forward of the mast].

I had a very narrow escape while standing on the quarter deck with Captain Forrester of the marines. The first lieutenant (the late Admiral Alexander Fraser) came up to us, and while speaking, a shot passed between us and stuck on the larboard [port] side of the quarter deck. We were very close at the time, so that it could only have been a few inches from us. It knocked the speaking-trumpet out of Fraser's hand and seemed to have electrified Captain Forrester and myself. . . .

A curious circumstance took place during the action. Two of the boys who had gone down for powder fell out in consequence of one attempting to take the box from the other, when a regular fight took place. It was laughable to see them boxing on the larboard side, and the ship in hot action on the starboard.[1] ■

PEOPLE

FOUND!

On 10 November 1871, in a remote area of Africa, newspaperman Henry M. Stanley met David Livingstone, a missionary of international fame who had been feared dead. Newspapers worldwide acclaimed the news! The encounter inspired Stanley to plead for missionaries: "Oh, that some pious, practical missionary would come here! . . . What a field and harvest ripe for the sickle of civilization. . . . It is the practical Christian tutor who can teach people how to become Christians, cure their diseases, construct dwellings. . . . You need not fear to spend money on such a mission." [2]

Stanley's comments brought an influx of missionaries to Africa in the closing decades of the nineteenth century.

A couple of hours brought us to the base of a hill, from the top of which the Kirangozi said we could obtain a view of the great Tanganyika Lake. Heedless of a rough path or of the toilsome steep, spurred onward by the cheery promise, the ascent was performed in a short time. I was pleased at the sight; and, as we descended, it opened more and more into view until it was revealed at last as a grand inland sea, bounded westward by an appalling and black-blue range of mountains and stretching north and south without bounds, a grey expanse of water. . . .

We are but a mile from Ujiji now, and it is high time we should let them know a caravan is coming; so "Commence firing" is the word passed along the length of the column, and gladly do they begin. They have loaded their muskets half full, and they roar like the broadside of a line-of-battle ship. Down go the ramrods, sending huge charges home to the breech, and volley after volley is fired. The flags are fluttered; the banner of America is in front, waving joyfully; the guide is in the zenith of his glory. The former residents of Zanzita will know it directly and will wonder—as well they may—as to what it means. Never were the Stars and Stripes so beautiful to my mind—the breeze of the Tanganyika has such an effect on them. The guide blows his horn, and the shrill, wild clangour of it is far and near; and still the cannon muskets tell the noisy seconds. By this time the Arabs are fully alarmed; the natives of Ujiji, Waguha, Warundi, Wanguana, and I know not whom hurry up by the hundreds to ask what it all means—this fusillading, shouting, and blowing of horns and flag flying. . . .

Suddenly a man—a black man—at my elbow shouts in English, "How do you do, sir?"

"Hello, who the deuce are you?"

"I am the servant of Dr. Livingstone," he says; and before I can ask any more questions he is running like a madman toward the town. . . .

As I come nearer, I see the white face of an old man among them. He has a cap with a gold band around it, his dress is a short jacket of red blanket cloth, and his pants—well, I didn't observe. I am shaking hands with him. We raise our hats, and I say:

"Dr. Livingstone, I presume?"[3] ∎

DISASTER

CITY CONSUMED

On 17 April 1906, a devastating earthquake hit San Francisco. The quake and its subsequent fires killed 452 people and left 225,000 homeless. Among the observers was the author Jack London.

San Francisco is gone! . . .

On Wednesday morning at a quarter past five came the earthquake. A minute later the flames were leaping upward. In a dozen different quarters south of Market Street, in the working class ghetto, and in the factories, fires started. There was no opposing the flames. There was no organization, no communication. All the cunning adjustments of a twentieth-century city had been smashed by the earthquake. The streets were humped into ridges and depressions and piled with debris of fallen walls. The steel rails were twisted into perpendicular and horizontal angles. The telephone and telegraph systems were disrupted. And the great water mains had burst. All the shrewd contrivances and safeguards of man had been thrown out of gear by thirty seconds' twitching of the earth's crust . . . .

Wednesday night saw the destruction of the very heart of the city. Dynamite was lavishly used, and many of San Francisco's proudest structures were crumbled by man himself into ruins, but there was no withstanding the onrush of the flames. Time and again successful stands were made by the firefighters, and every time the flames flanked around on either side, or came up from the rear, and turned to defeat the hard-won victory . . . .

On Thursday morning, at a quarter past five, just twenty-four hours after the earthquake, I sat on the steps of a small residence of Nob Hill. With me sat Japanese, Italians, Chinese, and Negroes—a bit of the cosmopolitan flotsam of the wreck of the city . . . .

I went inside with the owner of the house on the steps of which I sat. He was cool and cheerful and hospitable. "Yesterday morning," he said, "I was worth six hundred thousand dollars. This morning this house is all I have left. It will go in fifteen minutes." . . . .

I passed out of the house. Day was trying to dawn through the smoke pall. A sickly light was creeping over the face of things. Once only the sun broke through the smoke pall, blood-red and showing quarter its usual size. The smoke pall itself, viewed from beneath, was a rose color that pulsed and fluttered with lavender shades. Then it turned to mauve and yellow and dun [brownish dark gray]. There was no sun. And so dawned the second day on stricken San Francisco.[4] ■

■ EXPLORATION

A WHIFF OF HOSPITALITY

Two men provided the commentary for the last event, which occurred on 21 July 1969. The writers were Neil Armstrong, who took "one small step for a man, one giant leap for mankind," and his companion, Edwin Aldrin.

Neil Armstrong: Of all the spectacular views we had, the most impressive to me was on the way to the moon, when we flew through its shadow. We were still thousands of miles away, but close enough, so the moon almost filled our circular window. It was eclipsing the sun, from our position, and the corona of the sun was visible around the limb of the moon as a gigantic lens-shaped or saucer-shaped light, stretching out to several lunar diameters. It was magnificent, but the moon was even more so. We were in its shadow, so there was no part of it illuminated by the sun. It was illuminated only by earth shine.

I was really aware, visually aware, that the moon was in fact a sphere not a disc. It seemed almost as if it were showing us its roundness, its similarity in shape to our Earth, in a sort of welcome. I was sure that it would be a hospitable host. It had been awaiting its first visitors for a long time . . . .

Edwin Aldrin: The blue color of my boot has completely disappeared now into this—still don't know exactly what color to describe this other than grayish-cocoa color. It appears to be covering most of the lighter part of my boot . . . very fine particles . . . .

Odor is very subjective, but to me there was a distinct smell to the lunar material—pungent, like gunpowder or spent cap-pistol caps. We carted a fair amount of lunar dust back inside the vehicle with us, either on our suits and boots or on the conveyor system we used to get boxes and equipment back inside. We did notice the odor right away.[5] ■

Before we survey the concepts, foes, key figures, writers, and trends of the Modern Church Period, let's review what we have covered.

Self-Test

A. Complete the Arc of Church History.

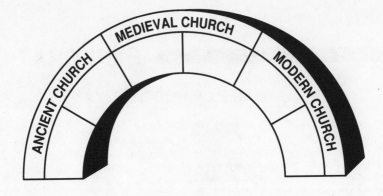

B. Complete the Story of Church History.

Period	Era	Date	Epoch	Pivotal Church Figure	Story Line
Ancient Church					Bishops _____ the churches as the congregations grew, developed distinct _____, and suffered _____.
					Theologians _____ the church, upheld its _____, and continued its _____ .
Medieval Church					Monks _____ the barbarians, transmitted and _____ culture, and _____ leadership.
					Reformers _____ the teachings and _____ of the church and called for _____.
Modern Church					Churchmen _____ over dogma, _____ new colonies, and contended with Enlightened _____.
					Strategists faced a shifting _____ _____ coped with social and political_____ , and found new ways to share their Christian faith at home and _____ .

❧ ❧ ❧

Tomorrow, we will begin our final survey of the Modern Church Period.

TWENTY-SIX

CONCEPTS: MODERN CHURCH PERIOD

T here once was a farmer who had several sons. "I'm an old man," the farmer said. "I want you to know that when I die, you will find your inheritance in the vineyard." When the farmer died, his sons combed the vineyard. They shoveled. They spaded. They tilled carefully among the vines, but they discovered no inheritance.

In time, however, their cultivation paid off: the vineyard began to thrive, and the sale of the grapes brought great wealth. Suddenly, the brothers realized that by persistently working together, they had found their inheritance.[1]

There was an "inheritance in the vineyard" for the Protestants of the Post-Reformation period, but instead of carefully tilling the soil, denominations carelessly ploughed up the fields they intended to sow. Between 1563 and 1789, religious differences sparked wars, persecution, and great intolerance. Gradually, Christians grew tired of the dissension and began to seek constructive ways to solve problems. Many solutions, such as religious toleration, social reform, and the separation of church and state, were first introduced as denominational distinctions.

The Denominational Church Era

I. The Outstanding Concept: The Great Awakening

The Great Awakening was a series of revivals that occurred in the American colonies between 1725 and 1760. (A parallel revival called the Evangelical or Methodist Revival began a decade later in the British Isles under the Wesley brothers and George White-field.) The Awakening began in New Jersey with the preaching of T. J. Frelinghuysen, a German Pietist, and took root in New England in 1734 under Jonathan Edwards. The most phenomenal year for the Awakening was 1740, when George Whitefield toured the colonies. Whitefield, who cooperated with all denominations, made the revival an intercolonial, interdenominational event.

While critics charged that Edwards and Whitefield elicited "enthusiasm" (an emotional, semihysterical response to the preaching) rather than true salvation, the Awakening yielded twenty-five to fifty thousand new church members, fostered an antislavery sentiment, spurred Indian evangelism, and prompted the founding of new schools: Princeton (1746), Brown (1764), and Dartmouth (1769).

SUMMARY

The outstanding concept of the Denominational Church Era was the _____ _____.

II. Summary of Other Important Concepts:

1. British religious movements

2. Denominations with Puritan roots

3. Pietism

1. British religious movements: Puritans, Separatists, Nonconformists, and Dissenters. Four important religious movements that developed in England were:

1. *Puritans.* Elizabeth I (1558–1603) decided that the Church of England would be Protestant in faith and episcopal, or bishop-ruled, in government. The decision displeased the Reformed (Calvinist) Protestants, who rejected all appearances of Roman Catholicism and favored a presbyterian, or elder-led, government. (Because the bishops were appointed by the monarch, the queen, who headed the Church of England, preferred to control bishops rather than dealing with elders, who were selected through congregational processes.) Those Protestants who remained in the English church and worked to "purify" it were called Puritans. Both Elizabeth and her successor, James I (1603–1625), opposed the Puritans. Elizabeth called them "fault-finders," but James was more high-handed: "I will make them conform themselves, or I will harry them out of the land, or else do worse."[2]

2. *Separatists.* Separatists were Puritans who left the Church of England and formed "gathered" churches, congregations comprised of consenting, adult believers. Under James I, many Separatists fled to Holland and the New World.

3. *Nonconformists.* In 1662, Parliament passed the Act of Uniformity, which reinstituted the Anglican church and required that all ministers submit to episcopal ordination and vow allegiance to the national church. Ministers who would not consent were called Nonconformists and were excluded from the church. Between 1662 and 1688, thousands of Nonconformists were arrested for their beliefs.

4. *Dissenters.* "Dissenter" was another name for Nonconformist.

During the seventeenth century, English society divided along religious lines: the poor were Dissenters or Nonconformists, the middle class were Puritans, and the aristocracy and gentry (untitled landowners) were Anglicans.

2. Denominations with Puritan roots: Presbyterians, Baptists, Congregationalists, and Quakers. Four English denominations, rooted in Puritan soil, strongly influenced the American colonies:

1. The *Presbyterians* originated with the Reformed churches, which were organized by John Knox in Geneva. The Presbyterians eventually resettled in England and Scotland and supported Puritan policies. During the English Civil War, a Puritan Parliament united the English and Scottish Presbyterian churches under the Westminster Confession (1648), the definitive statement of Presbyterian doctrine. In the American colonies, Presbyterian immigration centered in Long Island and East Jersey.

2. The *Baptists* were founded in 1608 by John Smyth, a Separatist who had been persecuted by James I and fled to Holland. Baptists practiced believer's baptism, a radical concept. They were prominent in Cromwell's army, but after the Restoration, they, like all Nonconformists, were persecuted. Many fled to Rhode Island.

3. *Congregationalists,* or Independents, were descendants of the Separatists. In 1582, Robert Browne formalized Congregationalist beliefs around the "gathered" church concept, which had no bishops or elders and left decision making to the congregation. The Pilgrim fathers who sailed on the Mayflower brought the congregational pattern to America.

4. The *Society of Friends* (Quakers) was founded in 1652 by the Puritan George Fox. Fox taught that Christians were guided by the Holy Spirit as they received the Inner Light, a divinely imparted assurance which left believers "trembling." Critics scoffed at the trembling Friends and called them "Quakers."

   Quakers had no sacraments, ceremonies, or ministers; men and women preached as they were inspired. Quakers swore no oaths and would not bear arms. They openly criticized other denominations and interrupted meetings. In retaliation, they were harassed, beaten, stoned, and murdered. To escape reprisals, many sought refuge in America, where they created a similar stir. Yet, Quakers pricked the social conscience and brought reform to prisons, the banking system, and commerce. Quakers opposed slavery in America before 1776.

3. Pietism: Lutheran renewal. During the seventeenth century, when the Lutheran faith had grown formal, cold, and lifeless, Philip Jacob Spener (1635–1705) called Lutherans to Pietism, a renewal movement. In 1675, Spener wrote *Pia Desideria* (Pious Longings) which formalized Pietism around the following principles:

1. Home Bible study, prayer, and fasting.

2. A cooperative spirit between laity and clergy.

3. A living faith at work in the community.

4. An end to Protestant disputes.

5. Education and training for clergy and congregations.

6. Preaching that focused on repentance and holy living.

Pietists were known for their deep love for Christ, their hymn writing, social work, and early missionary efforts.

Self-Test

A. The important concepts of the Denominational Church Era. (Match the concepts with the descriptive statements.)

Pietism   The Great Awakening   British religious movements
Denominations with Puritan roots

_____ A series of revivals in the American colonies.

_____ Presbyterians, Baptists, Congregationalists, and Quakers.

_____ A renewal movement that began in the Lutheran Church.

_____ Puritans, Separatists, Nonconformists, and Dissenters.

B. The outstanding concept of the Denominational Church Era. (Insert the name of the outstanding concept on the blank below.)

The outstanding concept of the Denominational Church Era was the _____ _____.

C. Wheel chart. (Place the name of the great concept on the wheel chart.)

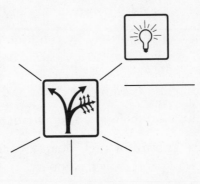

The Global Church Era

I. The Outstanding Concept: The Great Century of Protestant Missions

The nineteenth century was the "Great Century of Protestant Missions." The movement began with William Carey (1761–1834) and was sustained by mission societies, organizations that directed foreign evangelism. Among the early societies were the Baptist Missionary Society (1792), the London Mission Society (1795), and

the American Board of Commissioners for Foreign Missions
(1810).

Mission societies targeted four regions, which are listed below,
along with some of the leading missionaries for the areas.

Region	Leading Missionaries
India and Central Asia	William Carey and Adoniram Judson
The Pacific Islands	John Williams and Hiram Bingham
Africa	Robert Moffat and David Livingstone
The Far East	Robert Morrison and Hudson Taylor

By mid-century, three special groups of missionaries began to
join the ranks:

1. *Single, female missionaries* entered the field around 1860,
   when single women's mission societies were formed. Lottie
   Moon and Amy Carmichael were two noteworthy single missionaries.

2. *Faith missionaries* began serving in 1865 with Hudson
   Taylor's China Inland Mission. Faith missionaries received
   no set salary but literally lived "by faith."

3. *Student volunteer missionaries* originated with the Student Volunteer Movement (SVM), founded in 1886, by D. L. Moody
   and John Mott. Under the motto, "The evangelization of
   the world in this generation," the SVM placed more than
   twenty thousand college students in foreign missions.

SUMMARY

The outstanding concept of the Global Church Era
was _____ _____.

II. Summary of Other Important Concepts:

1. The Second Great Awakening

2. Ecumenism

3. Vatican II

1. The Second Great Awakening: The second American revival. The Second Great Awakening (1795–1835) was a two-phase series of revivals in the American colonies. The early phase (1795–1825) focused on the colleges and on the frontier. The later phase (1825–1835) centered on the preaching of Charles Finney (1792–1875), the "Father of American Revivalism." Finney used "new measures" to promote evangelism, such as praying for a person by name, inviting new believers to come forward, allowing women to pray, and organizing home visits. Finney also established the Benevolent Empire, a network of volunteer organizations—for example, the American Bible Society and the American Temperance Society—where Christians had opportunity to demonstrate their faith.

2. Ecumenism: The attempt to reunite Christians. The twentieth-century drive to unite Christian groups for cooperative action was called ecumenism. The modern ecumenical movement began in 1910, when John Mott organized the Edinburgh Missionary Conference, the first interdenominational missionary assembly. That meeting shaped the vision for a united modern church, strengthened the Federal Council of the Churches of Christ in America (later renamed the National Council of Churches), and paved the way for the World Council of Churches (1948). Both councils promoted social and political action from a theologically liberal viewpoint.

Currently, the World Council of Churches has 316 units with a combined total of 450 million people. All the major denominations are included except the Roman Catholic and the evangelical churches.

3. Vatican II: A conciliatory church council. When the Council of Trent anathematized the Protestants in 1563, it essentially closed a door on Catholic/Protestant cooperation that was not opened again until 1962, when Pope John XXIII convened Vatican II, the most recent Catholic church council.

Vatican II was the first council called to renew the church. It simplified worship (Mass in vernacular languages was permitted) and called for greater biblical knowledge and liturgical participation among Catholics. Vatican II encouraged dialogue with other Christians, who were called "separated brethren." Orthodox, Anglican, and Protestant observers attended the meetings. Although there were no changes in doctrine, the attitude and language of Vatican II was decidedly conciliatory.

Self-Test

A. The important concepts of the Global Church Era. (Match the concepts with the descriptive statements below.)

Ecumenism   Vatican II   The Second Great Awakening
The Great Century of Protestant Missions

_____ The drive to reunite the traditions of Christianity for cooperative action.

_____ Nineteenth-century global evangelism.

_____ The church council that encouraged openness between Catholic and non-Catholic Christians.

_____ A series of revivals in America that inspired social reform during the nineteenth century.

B. The outstanding concept of the Global Church Era. (Insert the name of the outstanding concept on the blank below.)

The outstanding concept of the Global Church Era
was _____ _____ .

C. Wheel chart. (Place the name of the great concept on the wheel chart.)

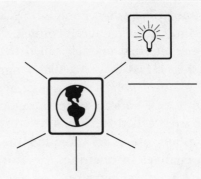

TWENTY-SEVEN

FOES: MODERN CHURCH PERIOD

A t an official reception during the Civil War, President Lincoln referred to the Southerners as erring human beings rather than as foes to be exterminated. An elderly lady, a fiery patriot, rebuked him for speaking kindly of his enemies when he ought to be thinking of destroying them. "Why, madam," said Lincoln, "do I not destroy my enemies when I make them my friends?"[1]

By 1550, the church had fought a lot of enemies: emperors, false teachers, Islamic invaders, and weak leadership. Through it all, the church had responded, adapted, recovered, and persevered.

Yet, during the Modern Church Period, new enemies called "isms" began gnawing at the foundations of Christianity. These isms—philosophies and ideologies—were hard to befriend. Some thwarted evangelism. Most contradicted Scripture. They sought to place man in control of the universe. The great minds were no longer questioning the jurisdiction of the pope or the authority of Scripture; they were debating the very existence of God.

Let's briefly identify some of the significant "isms" and their leading advocates.

The Denominational Church Era

I. Review:

Fill in the blanks to bring the wheel chart up to date.

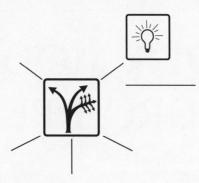

II. The Major Foe: Deism

Deism was a religion based on the belief that God had created the world, set laws in place to govern it, and then became indifferent to its functioning. Deists thought of God as a dispassionate watch-maker, who wound a clock and let it run. Deism denied the super-natural aspects of Christianity—the role and work of Jesus, the in-spiration of Scripture, prophecy, miracles, and prayer—but maintained that the Bible had ethical and moral value for society.

Many eminent Western thinkers were deists, among them Jean-Jacques Rousseau (1712–1778) and Francois-Marie Arouet (1694–1778), who is better known as Voltaire. The philosopher Rousseau extolled the beauty of nature, touted individualism, and taught that man was naturally good but that he had been corrupted by society. Voltaire, a gifted and prolific writer (his correspondence alone to-taled ten thousand letters!), was also an articulate spokesman for deism. He admired Christ but abhorred the petty squabbles and characteristic machinations of Christian leaders. Notwithstanding, Voltaire's goal was to manage religion, not to destroy it. He wrote: "If God did not exist, it would be necessary to invent him."[2]

Two leading deists in America were Thomas Paine and Thomas Jefferson. Paine defended deism in his book, *The Age of Reason*; Jefferson, the third president of the United States, was the principal author of the Declaration of Independence.

SUMMARY

The major foe of the Denominational Church Era was

_____.

III. Summary of Other Important Foes.

1. Rationalism

2. Empiricism

3. Freemasonry/Unitarianism

1. Rationalism: Acquiring knowledge by reason. Rationalism was a philosophy that developed on the continent of Europe. Rationalism maintained that reason (deductive thinking) was the basis of all knowledge and that man had the ability to discover truth on his own, without relying on divine revelation. Rationalism did not reject faith in God, but, depending on the philosopher-thinker, distanced man from God. The leading thinkers were the "Continental Rationalists"—Baruch Spinoza, a Jewish lens-grinder from Holland; G. W. Leibniz, a German Protestant theologian who developed calculus; and Rene Descartes, the French Catholic inventor of analytic geometry known for his conclusion: "I think; therefore I am."

2. Empiricism: Acquiring knowledge by experience. Empiricism, which developed in England as a response to rationalism, was another Enlightenment philosophy that embodied a wide range of thinking. Empiricism claimed that experience rather than reason was the source of all knowledge. Empiricism denied the supernatural and focused on the material, teaching that what is real can be experienced through the senses. The leading British empiricists were John Locke, George Berkeley, and David Hume. Among them, David Hume, the first skeptic, was most hostile to Christianity with his criticism of the biblical miracles.

3. Freemasonry and Unitarianism: Religions of the Enlightenment. Freemasonry and Unitarianism were religious organizations whose modern developments were encouraged by the philosophies of the Enlightenment. Freemasonry began in the twelfth century as a religious/professional fraternity for English masons. The fellowship was abolished in 1547 and later reestablished as a religious, civic, and educational organization with secret rites. Freemasonry spread throughout Europe and became a bulwark for deism.

Modern Unitarianism was grounded in rationalism and the thinking of the Englishman, John Biddle (1615–1662), who was called the "Father of Unitarianism." Unitarians denied the doctrine of the Trinity and the divinity of Jesus and the Holy Spirit. Their beliefs challenged the concept of hell and criticized the doctrines of the Fall and the Atonement. Unitarians substituted reason and experience for scriptural authority; they had no official creed.

Self-Test

A. Foes of the Denominational Church Era. (Write the foe next to its appropriate statement.)

Empiricism　　　　　　Rationalism　　　　　Deism
Freemasonry and Unitarianism

_____ Religions rooted in Enlightenment philosophies.

_____ The belief that knowledge is gained by experience.

_____ The religion in which God creates the world but remains indifferent to it.

_____ The belief that knowledge is gained by reason alone.

B. Major foe of the Denominational Church Era. (Insert the name of the major foe on the blank below.)

The major foe of the Denominational Church Era was

_____.

C. Wheel chart. (Place the name of the major foe on the wheel chart.)

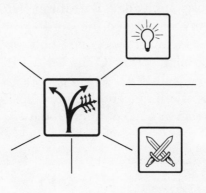

The Global Church Era

I. Review:

Fill in the blanks to bring the wheel chart up to date.

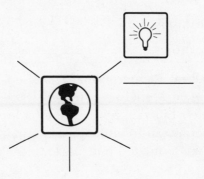

II. The Major Foe: Darwinism

Charles Darwin (1809–1882) was a naturalist, a field biologist, who turned the world upside down in 1859 with his publication, *The Origin of Species.* The book popularized the concepts of evolution and natural selection (survival of the fittest), set forth revolutionary ideas about the origin of life, and challenged the reliability of the Bible.

Reaction to Darwin's theory was strong and mixed. Anglican bishop Samuel Wilberforce ridiculed it. Baptist preacher Charles Spurgeon called it a "monstrous error," but T. H. Huxley, a noted British scientist, applauded Darwinism. Huxley, in fact, championed the theory and coined the word *agnostic* to skirt the issue of God as Creator. (An agnostic, one who is uncertain about the existence of God, might pray: "O my God, if there is a God, save my soul, if I have a soul.") *The Origin of Species,* the most controversial publication of the nineteenth century, sparked a debate between science and religion that continues today.

SUMMARY

The major foe of the Global Church Era was _____.

III. Summary of Other Important Foes:

1. Liberalism

2. Freudianism

3. Colonialism

1. Liberalism: Reinterpreting Historic Christianity. Liberalism, sometimes called Modernism, trailed Darwinism in the late nineteenth century. Liberals reinterpreted Christianity in light of science, philosophy, and contemporary culture and concluded that Christianity was outdated and irrelevant. To varying degrees, liberal theologians denied the authority of Scripture, searched for the "historical Jesus" (a figure other than the one portrayed in Scripture), espoused the fatherhood of God and the brotherhood of man, and focused on social reform and political action. Walter Rauschenbusch's "social gospel," Julius Wellhausen's "higher criticism," and Albert Schweitzer's "reverence for life" are manifestations of liberal thinking.

2. Freudianism: Inventing God to offset frustration. Sigmund Freud (1856–1939) laid the groundwork for modern psychology. He formulated a system for understanding human behavior based on the concepts of the unconscious mind, repressed desires, transference, dreams, and free association. Freud himself was an atheist who called religion a neurosis (a conflict between the different parts of the mind). For Freud, God was an invention conjured up within the mind to help it cope with frustration. Freud described God as a father figure and concluded: "The face which smiled at us in the cradle, now magnified to infinity, smiles down upon us from heaven."[3]

3. Colonialism: Dominating a foreign culture. Colonialism was the imperialistic practice whereby officials, "transplanted" from a dominant, usually distant nation, exerted control over another culture. A classic example was English colonialism in India, where the British government, via the East India Company, sought economic advantages. The East India Company, an English business conglomerate, was a powerful organization that engaged in diplomacy, maintained a military force, and acquired territory. The East India Company thwarted many of the early missionaries—William Carey, Adoniram Judson, and Robert Morrison—for fear that Christianity would upset local governments and affect trade relations.

Colonialism also hampered evangelistic efforts because missionaries, who sometimes presented Western-flavored Christianity, were viewed as extensions of the dominating government and were openly resented. This latent resentment was particularly strong in China, where, in 1900, scores of missionaries were slaughtered during an anti-Christian uprising called the Boxer Rebellion.

Self-Test

A. Foes of the Global Church Era. (Write the foe next to its appropriate statement.)

Darwinism   Freudianism   Liberalism
Colonialism

_____ The practice where officials "transplanted" from one nation exerted control over another culture.

_____ Espoused evolution and natural selection.

_____ Taught that God was an invention of the human mind.

_____ The movement which examined Christianity in light of science and modern culture.

B. Major foe of the Global Church Era. (Insert the name of the major foe on the blank below.)

The major foe of the Global Church Era was _____.

C. Wheel chart. (Place the name of the major foe on the wheel chart.)

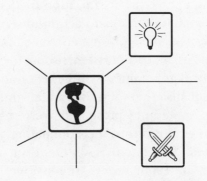

_____

TWENTY-EIGHT

KEY FIGURES: MODERN CHURCH PERIOD

C ircuit riders were those dauntless itinerant preachers who commuted around the English countrysides tending to scattered congregations. John Wesley was one of the best. What was life like for this energetic circuit rider? Step into the eighteenth century.

Between five and six, the coach called and took me to Mighton Car, about half a mile from the town. A huge multitude, rich and poor, horse and foot, with several coaches, were soon gathered together, to whom I cried with a loud voice and a composed spirit, "What shall it profit a man, if he shall gain the whole world and lose his own soul?" Some thousands of the people seriously attended, but many behaved as if possessed by Moloch [an Ammonite god who consumed first-born babies]. Clods and stones flew about on every side, but they neither touched nor disturbed me. When I had finished my discourse, I went to take coach, but the coachman had driven clear away. We were at a loss, till a gentlewoman invited my wife and me to come into her coach. She brought some inconveniences on herself thereby; not only as there were nine of us in the coach, but also as the mob closely attended us, throwing in at the windows whatever came next to hand. But a large gentlewoman who sat in my lap screened me so that nothing came near me.[1]

Not all the key figures of the Modern Church Period had such precarious experiences. They did, however, share a common bond: all found unique ways to incorporate the gospel into changing cultures, whether at home or around the world. Let's briefly survey the lives and contributions of eight modern Christians.

The Denominational Church Era

I. Review:

Fill in the blanks to bring the wheel chart up to date.

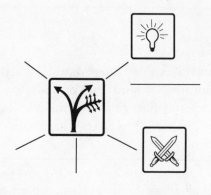

II. The Key Figure: John Wesley

John Wesley (1703–1791) never intended to start a denomination. He was an Anglican minister who preached to the working classes—coal miners, factory workers, and laborers—segments of society ignored by the Church of England.

Wesley believed that "the world was his parish" and used creative methods to reach his audience. He preached to people on their way to work—in fields, barns, and town squares. His sermons were lively, confrontational, and stressed conversion. He avoided heavy doctrine and focused on "heartfelt religion." Wesley and those who used this approach were called "methodists," although Wesley himself defined a Methodist as "one who lives according to the method laid down in the Bible."[2]

To ease Methodist converts into the Anglican church, John Wesley developed "societies," small groups that studied the Bible, prayed, sang, and encouraged social work. Methodist societies were organized into larger units; each was cared for by a circuit rider.

Methodism permeated English life. When Wesley died, one observer wrote: "By the humane endeavours of him [John Wesley] and his brother Charles a sense of decency in morals and religion was introduced to the lowest classes of mankind; the ignorant were instructed, the wretched relieved, and the abandoned reclaimed."[3]

Always practical, John Wesley lived by his *Rule for Christian Living*:

> Do all the good you can,
> By all the means you can,
> In all the ways you can,
> In all the places you can,
> At all the times you can,
> To all the people you can,
> As long as ever you can.[4]

Wesleyan Methodism was implanted in the American colonies during the 1760s by unofficial Methodist laypreachers. Francis Asbury, the great circuit rider and leader of American Methodism, came to America in 1771.

SUMMARY

The key figure of the Denominational Church Era was

_____ _____.

III. Summary of Other Important Figures:

1. Count Nikolaus Zinzendorf

2. Jonathan Edwards

3. George Whitefield

1. Count Nikolaus Zinzendorf: The founder of the Moravian Brethren. Nikolaus Zinzendorf (1700–1760) was a German Pietist who organized the Moravian Brethren Church from a refugee community called *Herrnhut* ("under the Lord's watch") that had settled on his property. The Moravians were known for their mystical faith ("heart" religion) and their zeal for evangelism. Missionaries from Herrnhut were in the West Indies, Greenland, Lapland, Georgia, Surinam, Africa, Algeria, Ceylon, Romania, Amsterdam, and Constantinople fifty years before William Carey sailed for India.

Moravians loved hymn singing. The count himself was a gifted, compulsive hymn writer. Once, while visiting New York, he became so preoccupied with writing verses that a justice of the peace fined him for breaking the Sabbath. In 1738, John Wesley visited Zinzendorf at Herrnhut and subsequently incorporated many Moravian practices into Methodism. In 1793, the mission policies of the Moravians inspired the Baptist Missionary Society, the first English missionary society.

2. Jonathan Edwards: The colonial theologian. Jonathan Edwards (1703–1758) was colonial America's greatest theologian. He championed orthodox Christianity against the Enlightenment philosophies and played a pivotal role in the Great Awakening as advocate, preacher, and observer. Edwards described the effects of the revival in *A Faithful Narrative of the Surprising Work of God* (1737):

> This work of God . . . and the number of true saints multiplied, soon made a glorious alteration in the town; so that in the spring and summer following, anno 1735, the town seemed to be full of the presence of God: it was never so full of love, nor of joy, and yet so full of distress, as it was then . . . . It was a time of joy in families on account of salvation being brought unto them.[5]

Edwards was born the same year as John Wesley; both men were close friends of George Whitefield. Jonathan Edwards delighted in John Wesley's hymnbooks, and Wesley supervised the English publication of Edwards's writings. The two men, however, never met.

3. George Whitefield: The great preacher of the Awakening. George Whitefield (1714–1770) was the greatest preacher of the Awakening. His relentless message was: "Ye must be born again!" Whitefield, an Anglican, roused congregations and ministers of all denominations. "The reason why congregations have been so dead," Whitefield exclaimed, "is because dead men preach to them."[6]

Whitefield enjoyed the friendship of Benjamin Franklin, who was amazed that the preacher could make his voice heard by thirty thousand people without the aid of amplification. Whitefield had an even closer relationship with John and Charles Wesley; all three had been students at Oxford and belonged to the Holy Club, a society for spiritual development. Whitefield was the first to be called a "Methodist." He developed many of the creative methods for evangelism that John Wesley later used.

Self-Test

A. Important figures of the Denominational Church Era. (Match the figures with their descriptive statements.)

Nikolaus Zinzendorf   John Wesley   Jonathan Edwards
George Whitefield

_____ Pietist founder of the Moravian Church.

_____ The greatest preacher of the Great Awakening.

_____ Used "methods"—societies, circuits, and open-air preaching.

_____ Colonial America's greatest theologian.

B. Key figure of the Denominational Church Era. (Insert the name of the key figure on the blank below.)

The key figure of the Denominational Church Era was

_____ _____.

C. Wheel chart. (Place the name of the key figure on the wheel chart.)

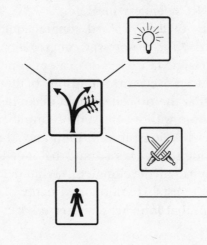

The Global Church Era

I. Review:

Fill in the blanks to bring the wheel chart up to date.

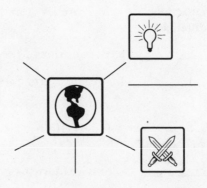

II. The Key Figure: Billy Graham

Evangelism captured the imagination of Billy Graham (1918-). "I had one passion, and that was to win souls. I didn't have a passion to be a great preacher. I had a passion to win souls."[7]

Billy Graham first received national attention in 1949 while conducting a city-wide revival in Los Angeles. In 1950, he organized the Billy Graham Evangelistic Association and honed his revival format. Large-scaled meetings, urban audiences, contemporary music, and outdoor stadiums became the ingredients for a Graham "crusade." At the heart of his ministry was a simple gospel message, punctuated by the oft-used phrase: "The Bible says . . . "

Billy Graham was interdenominational in approach. He sought the help of local ministers and church leaders. Graham trained all volunteers, provided counselors for inquirers, and followed up on decisions, incorporating new believers into local churches.

In 1954, Graham organized his First Greater London Crusade, and as a result, the Billy Graham crusades toured the world—the Far East, Australia, Africa, and South America. By the 1970s, Billy Graham was recognized worldwide as the unofficial spokesman for evangelical Christianity.

Besides the crusades, Billy Graham used other tools for evangelism: radio, television, and films. He wrote several best-selling books, including *Peace with God* (1952) and *World Aflame* (1965), and started two magazines, *Christianity Today* and *Decision*. Mr. Graham has also sponsored several international conferences on evangelism.

Billy Graham's personal integrity, his simple biblical messages, and his strategic use of technology have made him one of the most widely recognized and admired Christians in the world.

SUMMARY

The key figure of the Global Church Era was _____ _____ .

III. Summary of Other Important Figures:

1. William Carey

2. Charles Spurgeon

3. D. L. Moody

1. William Carey: The "Father of the Modern Missionary Movement." William Carey (1761–1834), a Baptist preacher from England, is called the "Father of the Modern Missionary Movement." Carey inspired the first mission society and set in place practices which became models for later missionary endeavors. He translated the Bible into six languages, built indigenous churches, established schools, and ran a print shop. Unlike some of the later missionaries, Carey worked hard to preserve the culture of India. Only with a few practices—suttee (burning a widow on the funeral pyre of her husband), infanticide, and child prostitution—did he seek reforms. Carey's life and work are a testimony to his belief: "Expect great things from God; attempt great things for God."

2. Charles Haddon Spurgeon: The greatest Victorian preacher. Charles Spurgeon (1834–1892) was the phenomenal preacher of the Metropolitan Tabernacle, Victorian England's most famous church. Ensconced in Scripture, Spurgeon bored away at sin with his melodic voice, dramatic timing, and superb command of the language, until all that was left was Jesus. Although critics called his sermons "vulgar and theatrical," crowds flocked to hear him. "I take my text," Spurgeon once commented, "and make a beeline to the Cross."[8] Collectively, Spurgeon's writings—his sermons, prayers, and books—comprise the largest set of written material by a single author in the history of Christian publishing. Spurgeon's most popular writing is *All of Grace*, which discusses salvation; the manuscript was the first book published by the Moody Press and remains its all-time best-seller.

3. D. L. Moody: The uneducated educator. D. L. Moody (1837–1899) became an international evangelist, but his early career was molded in the city of Chicago, where he was known as "Crazy Moody," the homespun preacher with a fervor for Sunday school. Moody was an uneducated, never-ordained, shoe salesman who invested his life in the "next generation." Moody preached, but he also started schools—Northfield School, Mt. Hermon School, and Moody Bible Institute, a church—the Illinois Street Church, a printing company—the forerunner of Moody Press, and held summer Bible conferences at his home in Massachusetts. "When I am gone," Moody once said, "I shall leave some grand men and women behind."[9] Modern statistics support his prediction. In 1989, one out of every ten missionaries from North America was a graduate of Moody Bible Institute.

Self-Test

A. Important figures of the Global Church Era. (Match the figures with their descriptive statements.)

Billy Graham   Charles Spurgeon   D. L. Moody
William Carey

_____ Father of "the Modern Missionary Movement."

_____ Victorian England's greatest preacher.

_____ The evangelist who promoted schools and training.

_____ The unofficial spokesman for evangelical Christianity.

B. Key figure of the Global Church Era. (Insert the name of the key figure on the blank below.)

The key figure of the Global Church Era was_____
_____.

C. Wheel chart. (Place the name of the key figure on the wheel chart.)

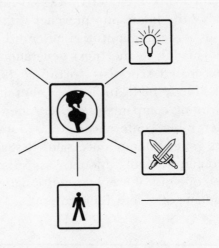

TWENTY-NINE

WRITERS/WRITINGS: MODERN CHURCH PERIOD

G eorge M. Cohan (1878–1942), the actor, songwriter, and playwright, had an unusual way of meeting his deadlines. Whenever he had a manuscript due, Cohan would hire an entire Pullman car drawing room and ride the train until he finished his work. Using this method, Cohan could turn out one hundred forty pages a night.[1]

None of the important writers of the Modern Church Period had the expensive habit of writing in a Pullman car, but many of the manuscripts were produced under unusual circumstances. One book was written in exile; another, in jail. An Oxford professor wrote for children, and a blind man wrote an epic poem. Two of the selected writings were group efforts, with a combined authorship of 114 men. Step through these modern entries and enjoy the diversity and familiarity of the period.

The Denominational Church Era

I. Review:

Fill in the blanks to bring the chart up to date.

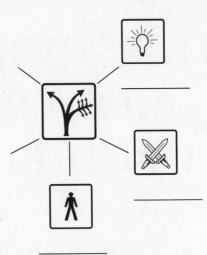

II. The Key Writing: The King James Bible

When James I became king of England in 1603, the Puritans requested a number of changes in Anglican worship. James dismissed every request except the one for a new translation of the Bible. Why a new Bible?

The Church of England used the Bishops' Bible, which the people did not like; and the people used the Geneva Bible, which the king did not like. A compromise seemed good. (James's admirers called him the "British Solomon.") James ordered "special pains taken for a uniform translation, which should be done by the best learned in both universities, then reviewed by the bishops, presented to the Privy Council, lastly ratified by royal authority, to be read in the whole Church, and no other."[2]

Beginning in 1607, fifty scholars worked nearly three years to create the King James Bible, which is also referred to as the King

James Version (KJV). Technically, the King James Bible is not a version, that is, a translation from the original texts; rather, the King James Bible is a revision of an earlier translation.

When the King James Bible was first issued in 1611, critics charged that its language was "archaic." Yet, the language provided the rhythm, cadence, and majesty that made the verses memorable, even into the twentieth century. *Christian History* recently stated: "Today . . . most people who can quote the Bible quote a version published in 1611."[3]

SUMMARY

The key writing of the Denominational Church Era was the

_____ _____ _____.

III. Summary of Other Important Writings:

1. *Foxe's Book of Martyrs*

2. *Paradise Lost*

3. *Pilgrim's Progress*

1. *Foxe's Book of Martyrs:* The Who's Who of Christian martyrs. John Foxe (1516–1587) lived through turbulent times under England's Henry VIII and his offspring. As a student, Foxe developed an insatiable curiosity about church history. His studies led him to espouse anti-Catholic views, opinions which forced him to flee for his life during the reign of the Catholic queen, Mary I (1553–1558). While exiled in Europe, he wrote *Foxe's Book of Martyrs,* a history written in Latin about the martyrs of Christianity.

After Elizabeth I ascended the throne, Foxe returned to England and in 1563 issued an English translation of the *Book of Martyrs.* The popular publication affirmed the Puritan belief that God directed the national destiny of England, much as He guided Israel after the Exodus. This belief infused Puritans with a sense of spiritual responsibility for the world; in America, the New England Puritans became the most faithful colonists to evangelize the Indians.

Among the many individuals affected by *Foxe's Book of Martyrs* was Charles Spurgeon, who recommended the book as "the perfect Christmas gift for a child."

2. *Paradise Lost:* The greatest poem of Puritanism. *Paradise Lost,* written in 1667 by John Milton, is the greatest poem of Puritanism and one of the two major epics of English literature. (*Beowulf* is the other.) John Milton was a scholarly man who wrote for an educated audience. His regular job was answering diplomatic letters in Latin, the official language of the English government.

Using concepts from the classical epics, Dante, the Bible, and Puritan theology, Milton wove into *Paradise Lost* the account of man's creation and expulsion from Eden, along with the saga of Satan and his determination to contend with God. Milton's prayer and purpose for the poem were clearly stated in the opening lines:

> . . . what in me is dark
> Illumine, what is low raise and support;
> That to the highth of this great argument
> I may assert Eternal Providence,
> And justify the ways of God to men. 1.22–26

Milton had been blind for fifteen years when he dictated *Paradise Lost* to one of his daughters.

3. *Pilgrim's Progress:* The number two best-seller in Christian publishing. John Bunyan (1628–1688) was a self-educated Nonconformist preacher who published more than sixty works. His most famous book was *Pilgrim's Progress* (1678), which was written while Bunyan was in jail for preaching. Next to the Bible, *Pilgrim's Progress* is the most popular book in the history of Christian publishing.

Pilgrim's Progress is an allegory, a story overlaid with symbolic meaning. It tells the tale of a hero named Christian who made a spiritual journey to the Celestial City. The story, filled with unforgettable characters and places—for example, Mr. Worldly Wiseman and the Slough of Despond—began as a dream. Here are the opening lines:

> As I walked through the wilderness of this world, I lighted on a certain place and laid me down to sleep; and as I slept, I dreamed a dream.
>
> I dreamed that I saw a man, with his face turned away from his own house—a book in his hand, and a great burden on his back. I looked and saw him open the book and read therein; and, as he read, he wept and trembled; and not being able to contain himself, he broke out with a lamentable cry, saying:
> *What shall I do to be saved?* [4]

Self-Test

A. Important writings of the Denominational Church Era. (Match the writing to the correct statement.)

The King James Bible   *Paradise Lost*   *Foxe's Book of Martyrs*
Pilgrim's Progress

_____ Published in 1611, it was the work of fifty scholars.

_____ The story of Christian and his journey to the Celestial City.

_____ The greatest poem of Puritanism.

_____ A Who's Who of Christian martyrs.

B. Key writing of the Denominational Church Era. (Insert the name of the key writing on the blank below.)

The key writing of the Denominational Church Era was the

_____ _____ _____.

C. Wheel chart. (Place the name of the key writing on the wheel chart.)

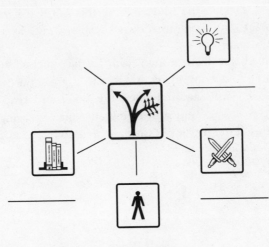

The Global Church Era

I. Review:

Fill in the blanks to bring the wheel chart up to date.

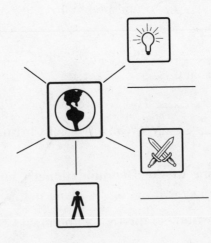

II. The Key Writer: C. S. Lewis

Although C. S. Lewis (1898–1963) was an atheist as a youth, he became the finest Christian apologist of the twentieth century. Cultured, witty, logical, and relevant, Lewis had "the rare gift of making righteousness readable." He was often called "the Apostle to the Skeptics." Between the time Lewis embraced Christianity in 1931 and his death in 1963, he wrote forty books dealing with the Christian faith, several of them for children. In addition, he was a highly regarded English professor at both Oxford and Cambridge.

Through his Christian writings, Lewis evangelized, instructed, nurtured, and entertained; his genius is best sampled. In *The Screwtape Letters,* one of Lewis' most popular books, Screwtape, a senior devil, advises Wormwood, his fledgling nephew, on how to separate a new Christian from God (whom Screwtape calls "the Enemy"):

> But do remember, the only thing that matters is the extent to which you separate the man from the Enemy. It does not matter how small the sins are, provided that their cumulative effect is to edge the man away from the Light and out into the Nothing. Murder is no better than cards if cards can do the trick. Indeed, the safest road to Hell is the gradual one—the gentle slope, soft underfoot, without sudden turnings, without milestones, without signposts.[5]

Other well-known books by C. S. Lewis are: the Space Trilogy, *The Problem of Pain,* the Chronicles of Narnia, *Mere Christianity, Surprised by Joy,* and *Till We Have Faces* (the work Lewis considered his finest novel). With more than forty million books in print, C. S. Lewis is the best-selling Christian author of all time.

SUMMARY

The key writer of the Global Church Era was _____ _____.

III. Summary of Other Important Writers or Writings:

1. *An Enquirey into the Obligation of Christians to Use Means for the Conversion of the Heathens*

2. *The Fundamentals*

3. Francis Schaeffer

1. *An Enquirey:* The charter for modern missions. William Carey (1761–1834) wrote *An Enquirey* in 1792 to convince his local English Baptist association to sponsor missions. The book included several mission-related topics, such as the scriptural justification for missions, a historical review of missionary efforts from the apostles to the Moravians, and a contemporary analysis of the countries of the world. Carey added a special section relating to the "heathens": "Their distance from us, their barbarous and savage way of living, the danger of being killed by them, the difficulty of procuring the necessaries of life . . . the unintelligibleness of their languages."[6] *An Enquirey* ended with a detailed strategy for missions work, including financial and prayer support, denominational cooperation, and the qualifications for missionary candidates.

Although *An Enquirey* was not well received initially, the book became "the charter of modern missions" as Carey lived out his plan.

2. *The Fundamentals:* A twentieth-century best-seller. *The Fundamentals* was a twelve-volume set of paperback books, published between 1910 and 1915. The set was written: (1) to oppose modernism and (2) to reaffirm the central truths of Christianity. Writers focused on the doctrines that were under attack, issues such as the virgin birth of Christ, His atonement and substitutionary death, and the inerrancy of Scripture.

The sixty-four writers of the series included: B. B. Warfield (1851–1921), a Presbyterian theologian; R. A. Torrey (1856–1928), the first superintendent of the Moody Bible Institute; and H. C. G. Moule (1841–1920), an English theologian associated with the Keswick Convention.

The Fundamentals was sent, free of charge, to more than three million seminary students, ministers, and missionaries. Those who adhered to the teachings were called "fundamentalists." During the 1920s and 1930s differences of opinion between fundamentalists and modernists divided several Protestant denominations.

3. Francis Schaeffer: The theologian who understood modern spiritual struggles. Francis Schaeffer (1912–1984), a twentieth-century theologian, is best remembered as the founder of L'Abri, a "shelter" for people grappling with spiritual struggles.

Schaeffer understood spiritual struggles. He himself went through several crises which prompted him to reexamine his beliefs about historical Christianity. "As I rethought my reasons for being a Christian, I saw again that there were totally sufficient reasons to know that the infinite-personal God does exist and that Christianity is true."[7]

Schaeffer's conclusions led him to establish L'Abri, where he taught, counseled, and emphasized the "Lordship of Christ in the totality of life." In addition, he wrote twenty-three books that were translated into more than twenty-five languages. Among his widely read titles are *The God Who Is There, Genesis in Space and Time, No Little People,* and *How Should We Then Live?*. Francis Schaeffer spent his later years developing films, such as *Whatever Happened to the Human Race?*, and motivating discussions among Christians about contemporary issues, such as abortion, civil rights, and euthanasia.

Self-Test

A. Important writers/writings of the Global Church Era. (Match the writer/writing to the correct statement.)

An Enquirey   C. S. Lewis   Francis Schaeffer
The Fundamentals

_____ Founded L'Abri.

_____ The paperback series written to oppose modernism.

_____ The best-selling Christian author of all time.

_____ The "charter for modern missions."

B. Key writer of the Global Church Era. (Insert the name of the key writer on the blank below.)

The key writer of the Global Church Era was _____

_____.

C. Wheel chart. (Place the name of the key writer on the wheel chart.)

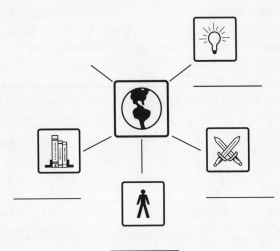

THIRTY

TRENDS: MODERN CHURCH PERIOD

I n his poem from *Partial Accounts,* William Meredith describes the struggle we all experience in expressing ourselves:

About Opera

It's not the tunes, although as I get older
Arias are what I hum and whistle.
It's not the plots—they continue to bewilder
In the tongue I speak and in several that I wrestle.

An image of articulateness is what it is:
Isn't this how we've always longed to talk?
Words as they fall are monotone and bloodless
But they yearn to take the risk these noises take.

What dancing is to the slightly spastic way
Most of us teeter through our bodily life
Are these measured cries to the clumsy things we say,
In the heart's duresses, on the heart's behalf.[1]

Those of us who pray share the poet's struggle. Our words fall "monotone and bloodless." After all, aren't they ordinary words—the ones we use to coax a child or implore our spouse? We know no special God vocabulary.

Our prayers begin all right, but somewhere about the fifth sentence, the focus darts off, intercepted like a missile. We're adults—grown up. So, it surprises us that we're not in better control. We communicate with the vet and the girl who slices cheese in the deli, but the truth is: We don't always communicate well with God.

We long to present "an image of articulateness" and so, like thousands of pray-ers before us, we borrow words. We quietly dip into Paul: Lord, help me set my mind on things above, not on the things that are on earth. We plead along with Moses: Confirm for me the work of my hands. We echo David: Create in me a clean heart.

Sometimes, "in the heart's duresses," we steal comfort from Isaiah. We need to know, we need to hear that the Everlasting God, the Lord, the Creator of the ends of the earth does not become weary or tired. In the process, we're assured, if only for an instant, that we have touched the mind of God, and after the last "Amen," what lingers are not puny pleas, but the truths we've borrowed.

The church has long searched for new and fresh ways to articulate the truths of Christianity. In the Denominational Church Era, this trend toward articulation focused on music. In the Global Church Era, the trend emphasized the dissemination of Scripture using technology. Let's examine these important trends as we close our study.

The Denominational Church Era

I. Review:

Fill in the blanks to bring the wheel chart up to date.

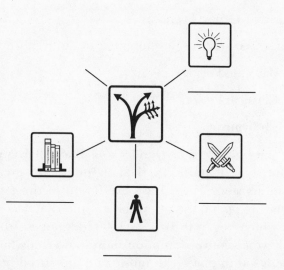

II. The Dominant Trend: Church Music

Classical music may seem remote, highbrow, or snobbish. But, if you've ever hummed "A Mighty Fortress Is Our God" or the "Hallelujah Chorus," you're a classicist. Classical music is vocal or instrumental music that is written in a set style for a concert, a religious service, an opera, or a ballet. Modern classical music includes three kinds of instrumental music—solo, chamber, and orchestral music—and four kinds of vocal music—songs, choral music, operas, and oratorios. Two important periods in music history occurred during the Denominational Church Era: the Baroque Period (1600–1750) and the Classical Period (1700–1800). Both affected the music of the Church.

SUMMARY

The dominant trend in the Denominational Church Era
was _____ _____.

III. Summary of Other Trends:

Let's look at three areas of development in modern Church music:

1. The Baroque Period

2. The Classical Period

3. English hymns

1. The Baroque Period: Handel and Bach. Baroque refers to
an elaborate style of music marked by grandeur, great contrast,
and dynamic tension. These traits are found in three popular baroque forms: the opera, the oratorio, and the cantata.

Opera, which began in Italy in 1600, developed from the idea
that a single voice conveys emotion more powerfully than multiple
voices. Opera was drama set to music and enhanced by new, glitzy
features, such as an orchestra, dancing, musical overtures, lavish
costumes, and imaginative scenery. Opera, with its actor-singers,
arias (solo songs), choruses, and recitatives (a style of narration
halfway between speaking and singing), offered "an image of articulateness" that spread quickly throughout Europe.

Since opera was too elaborate for church presentations, the
oratorio—religious drama set to music—was born. The oratorio
used recitatives, arias, and choruses but involved no acting or scenery. A short oratorio was called a cantata.

Among the Baroque composers who wrote sacred music were
George Frederic Handel (1685–1759), who is best remembered for
his oratorio, the *Messiah,* and Johann Sebastian Bach (1685–1750),
the organ virtuoso who also composed hundreds of cantatas,
among them "I Was in Much Tribulation" and "A Mighty Fortress
Is Our God." Bach's death concluded the Baroque Period.

2. The Classical Period: Haydn, Mozart, and Beethoven. During the Classical Period, chamber and orchestral music thrived, the piano supplanted the harpsichord, and the sonata form evolved as the blueprint for the symphony. Vocal music matured and comic opera, with its scintillating satire, was born.

Although classical composers wrote less church music than their predecessors, there were several noteworthy composers and compositions. Franz Joseph Haydn (1732–1809) was inspired by Handel's *Messiah* to write the magnificent oratorio, *The Creation,* which was based on the book of Genesis and *Paradise Lost.* Wolfgang Amadeus Mozart (1756–1791) wrote sixty sacred pieces, including his famous *Requiem.* Ludwig van Beethoven (1770–1827) composed the oratorio, *Christ on the Mount of Olives,* and the very familiar "Hymn to Joy."

3. English Hymns: Watts, Wesley, and Newton. While the Renaissance had created a popular interest in music, it was not until the end of the seventeenth century that English musicians began to write contemporary hymns. Modern hymns were paraphrases of Scripture or "hymns of human composure"—personal responses to biblical teachings.

Many writers contributed to the development of the English hymn. Thomas Ken (1637–1711) was one of the first to produce texts that were not simply versifications of the psalms. His famous refrain, the "Doxology," is still sung today. Isaac Watts (1674–1748), the "Father of English Hymnody," modernized the language of the psalms and pioneered songs of human composure, such as "When I Survey the Wondrous Cross." The hymns of Charles Wesley (1707–1788) were not only paraphrases of Scripture but paraphrases of the *Book of Common Prayer,* doctrine, and Christian experiences. John Newton (1725–1807), the former slave trader, wrote a collection of hymns called *Olney Hymns Hymnal,* which included the song "Amazing Grace" describing his own conversion. Augustus Toplady (1740–1778) wrote "Rock of Ages" to present doctrine.

Self-Test

A. Trends of the Denominational Church Era. (Match the terms to their descriptions.)

Church music   The Classical Period   English hymns
The Baroque Period

_____ A form of classical music.

_____ Haydn, Mozart, and Beethoven.

_____ Handel and Bach: opera, oratorio, and the cantata.

_____ Watts, Wesley, and Newton.

B. Dominant trend summary. (Fill in the blanks with the correct answer.)

The dominant trend in the Denominational Church Era was

_____ _____.

C. Wheel chart. (Place the dominant trend on the wheel chart.)

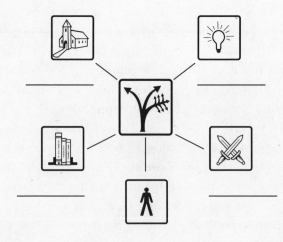

The Global Church Era

I. Review:

Fill in the blanks to bring the wheel chart up to date.

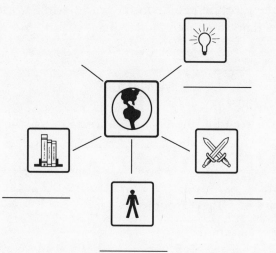

II. The Dominant Trend: The Dissemination of the Bible

As early as 1802, Christians were clamoring for Bibles to distribute at home and on mission fields. The first Bible society, the British and Foreign Bible Society, was established in 1804 in response to the pleas of a Methodist minister for Welsh Bibles. The American Bible Society followed in 1816 and initially targeted the frontier— Kentucky, Tennessee, and Illinois—European immigrants, and the American Indians.

Bible societies oversaw the translation, publication, and distribution of Bibles. The agencies, which guided missionaries as they translated, undertook the printing of Scriptures but left the actual distribution to local churches. Bible societies were successful because they were nondenominational and produced low-cost translations "without doctrinal note or comment." In 1946, the major Bible societies of the world joined forces under the banner, United Bible Societies (UBS).

UBS, which tracks translation work worldwide, recently reported that at the beginning of the twentieth century, portions of Scripture were available in only sixty-seven of the world's fifty-one hundred languages. By 1990, there was at least one book of the Bible published in 1,946 languages—the languages used by more than 97 percent of the people in the world, while work has continued in more than one thousand languages.

SUMMARY

The major trend in the Global Church Era was the _____ of the_____.

III. Summary of Other Trends:

1. Bible translation

2. Modern language Bibles

3. Twentieth-century innovations

1. Bible translation: Wycliffe Bible Translators. One of the preeminent leaders in modern Bible translation work was Cam Townsend (1896–1982), the founder of Wycliffe Bible Translators (WBT) and the Summer Institute of Linguistics (SIL). Cam Townsend lived by one philosophy: "The greatest missionary is the Bible in the Mother tongue. It never needs a furlough, is never considered a foreigner."[2] Townsend founded WBT in 1934 and dedicated the organization to reducing all the languages of the world to writing and translating at least one Bible book into those languages. WBT promotes translation work among churches, secures financial support, and screens potential translators. SIL, the sister organization of WBT, provides intensive, linguistic training, supervises field work, and maintains relations with host governments. With a staff of over forty-two hundred, WBT has become the largest independent mission agency in church history.

2. Modern language Bibles: Good news for modern man. By the twentieth century, scholars, theologians, and linguists began to reexamine the Bible in light of newly found manuscripts and advances in linguistics. Protestants issued the American Standard Version (1901) and Catholics produced the Layman's New Testament (1928). The real proliferation of modern Bibles, called "modern speech translations," however, occurred after World War II, and many of the modern translations were sponsored by Bible societies.

Among the best-sellers were the following translations: The New Testament in Modern English (1958) by J. B. Phillips; the New American Standard Bible (1967); The Living Bible (1971), a paraphrase by Kenneth Taylor; Today's English Version: Good News Bible (1976); the New International Version (1978); and the Jerusalem Bible (1966), a result of Catholic scholarship. Also noteworthy were the International Children's Bible and the Bible in Basic English, both of which were created for readers with limited vocabularies.

Sample a modern language translation—the first four verses of Psalm 23 from the International Children's Bible:

> The Lord is my shepherd.
> I have everything I need.
> He gives me rest in green pastures.
> He leads me to calm water.
> He gives me new strength.
> For the good of his name,
> he leads me on paths that are right.
> Even if I walk through a very dark valley,
> I will not be afraid because you are with me.
> Your rod and your walking stick comfort me.[3]

The most recent addition to the family of modern language Bibles has been the Contemporary English Version (CEV) of the New Testament, a translation designed for listening. Introduced by the American Bible Society in 1991, CEV translators produced a modern language Bible written in a conversational style. Compare the opening lines of Matthew 6:[4]

Revised Standard Version	Contempory English Version
"Beware of practicing your piety before men in order to be seen by them. . . . Thus, when you give alms, sound no trumpet before you as the hypocrites do."	"When you do good deeds, don't try to show off. . . . When you give to the poor, don't blow a loud horn. That's what showoffs do."

3. Twentieth-century innovations: Technology shares the gospel.
Christianity has used many modern tools to disseminate the gospel.
Two principal vehicles have been radio, beginning in the 1920s,
and television in the 1950s. Under the direction of Christian broadcasting pioneers like Paul Rader in Chicago and Clarence Jones in
Ecuador, radio established a Christian witness that time has not diminished. According to 1980 figures released by the National Religious Broadcasters, there are 1450 Christian radio and television
stations in the world.

Religious television broadcasting peaked in the 1980s with such
well-known personalities as Pat Robertson, Robert Schuller, Jimmy
Swaggart, and Jerry Falwell. Although television can lead to an
"electronic church" mentality and recent financial mishandlings
have brought scandal, television remains, in responsible hands, a
viable tool for evangelism. Modern evangelism has also been aided
by magazines, newspapers, films, correspondence schools, cassette
tapes, computers, and aviation.

Self-Test

A. Trends of the Global Church Era. (Match the terms to their descriptions.)

Bible societies   Modern language Bibles   Bible translation
Twentieth-century innovations

_____ Work associated with Cam Townsend.

_____ Radio, television, films, tapes, and aviation.

_____ Nineteenth-century agencies which supervised the translation, publication, and distribution of Bibles.

_____ New International Version, The Living Bible, and the International Children's Bible.

B. Dominant trend summary. (Fill in the blanks below with the correct answer.)

The major trend in the Global Church Era was the _____ of the _____.

C. Wheel chart. (Place the dominant trends on the wheel chart.)

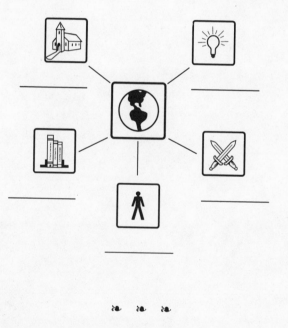

≥ ≥ ≥

Congratulations! You have now completed *30 Days To Understanding Church History.* May you use your newly acquired knowledge to broaden your spiritual heritage.

NOTES

Chapter 1: Time and History

1. Stephen Dunning, Edward Lueders, Hugh Smith, "Ancient History," *Reflections on a Gift of Watermelon Pickle . . .* (New York: Scholastic Book Services, 1966), 63.

Chapter 2: Eras, Epochs, and Dates

1. Clifton Fadiman, *The Little, Brown Book of Anecdotes* (Boston, Massachusetts: Little, Brown and Company, 1985), 122.

Chapter 4: Geography: Ancient Church Period

1. Gauls, as quoted by Will Durant, *Caesar and Christ* (New York: Simon and Schuster, 1944), 471.

Chapter 5: Story Line: Infant Church Era

1. Frank Elia, interview with author, Pine Mountain, Georgia, December 6, 1989.
2. Christians, as quoted by Jean Comby, *How to Read Church History,* vol. I (New York: The Crossroad Publishing Company, 1989), 36.
3. Christians, as quoted by Dr. Tim Dowley, ed., *Eerdman's Handbook to the History of Christianity* (Hertfordshire, England: Lion Publishing, 1977), 69.
4. Ibid., 72.

Chapter 6: Story Line: Adolescent Church Era

1. John Keats, *The International Thesaurus of Quotations* (New York: Thomas Y. Crowell Company, 1970), 1064:32.

2. Constantine, as quoted by Dowley, *Eerdman's*, 130.
3. Donatus, as quoted by Dowley, *Eerdman's*, 203.

Chapter 7: Headlines: Ancient Church Period

1. *Collier's Encyclopedia*, 1966 ed., s.v. "Newpaper."
2. Titus, as quoted by Durant, *Caesar*, 289.
3. Juvenal, *Bartlett's Familiar Quotations* (Boston: Little, Brown and Company, 1980), 122.
4. Durant, *Caesar*, 635.

Chapter 8: Concepts: Ancient Church Period

1. Fadiman, *Little*, 576.

Chapter 9: Foes: Ancient Church Period

1. Fadiman, *Little*, 107.
2. Tacitus, as quoted by Dowley, *Eerdman's*, 71.
3. William Byron Forbush, ed., *Foxe's Book of Martyrs* (Grand Rapids, Michigan: Zondervan, 1926), 61.
4. Edward Gibbon, *The Decline and Fall of the Roman Empire*, vol.1 (New York: Modern Library, n.d.), 67.
5. Mark Galli, "The Persecuting Emperors," *Christian History* (August 1990): 21.
6. Philip Schaff, *History of the Christian Church*, vol. 2 (Grand Rapids, Michigan: Wm. B. Eerdman's Publishing Company, 1910), 60.
7. Eusebius, *The Ecclesiastical History* (Grand Rapids, Michigan: Baker Book House, 1955), 255.
8. Bruce L. Shelley, *Church History in Plain Language* (Dallas: Word Publishing, 1982), 114.
9. Terry L. Miethe, *The Compact Dictionary of Doctrinal Words* (Minneapolis, Minnesota: Bethany House Publishers, 1988), 147–8.
10. St. Augustine, "Fighting Isms and Schisms," *Christian History* (August 1987), 29.
11. Shelley, *Church History*, 127.

Chapter 10: Key Figures: Ancient Church Period

1. J. B. Lightfoot and J. R. Harmer, *The Apostolic Fathers*, 2nd ed. (Grand Rapids, Michigan: Baker Book House, 1989), 113.

2. Ibid., 103.
3. Ibid., 139.
4. Shelley, *Church History*, 118.

Chapter 11: Writers/Writings: Ancient Church Period

1. *First Apology*, as quoted by Dowley, *Eerdman's*, 127.
2. Tertullian, as quoted by Dowley, *Eerdman's*, 72.
3. Jerome, as quoted by Durant, *Caesar*, 614.
4. Dowley, *Eerdman's*, 188.
5. Eusebius, *Ecclesiastical History*, 13.
6. Confessions, Book X, as quoted by Roland H. Bainton, *The Church of Our Fathers* (Philadelphia: The Westminster Press, 1950), 60.
7. Ibid, Book I.

Chapter 12: Trends: Ancient Church Period

1. Dunning, *Reflection*, 104.
2. Bainton, *The Church*, 33–34.
3. Kenneth W. Osbeck, *101 More Hymn Stories* (Grand Rapids, Michigan: Kregel Publications, 1985), 243.
4. Will Durant, *The Age of Faith* (New York: Simon and Schuster, 1950), 130.

Chapter 13: Geography: Medieval Church Period

1. Durant, *Age*, 302.
2. Will Durant, *The Reformation* (New York: Simon and Schuster, 1957), 344.
3. Ibid.

Chapter 14: Story Line: Roman Church Era

1. Durant, *Age*, 464.

Chapter 15: Story Line: Reformation Church Era

1. Durant, *Reformation*, 285.
2. Fernand Braudel, *The Structures of Everyday Life*, vol. I (New York: Harper and Row, Publishers, 1981), 222.
3. Ibid., 221.
4. Durant, *Age*, 908.

5. Braudel, *Structures,* 400.
6. Durant, *Reformation,* 159.

Chapter 16: Headlines: Medieval Church Period

1. Durant, *Age,* 302.
2. Durant, *Age,* 371.
3. Books, as quoted by Durant, *Age,* 237.
4. Durant, *Age,* 298.
5. Durant, *Age,* 995.
6. Nicole Duplaix, "Fleas," *National Geographic* (May 1988): 678.
7. Ibid.
8. Ibid.
9. Durant, *Reformation,* 64.
10. Duplaix, "Fleas," 678.
11. Duplaix, "Fleas," 677.
12. Duplaix, "Fleas," 679.
13. Duplaix, "Fleas," 680–1.
14. Charles Panati, *Extraordinary Origins of Everyday Things* (New York: Harper and Row Publishers, 1987), 85.
15. Panati, *Extraordinary,* 86.
16. Carpini, as quoted by Durant, *Age,* 339.

Chapter 17: Concepts: Medieval Church Period

1. Shelley, *Church,* 258.
2. Durant, *Reformation,* 897.

Chapter 18: Foes: Medieval Church Period

1. Robert Hendrickson, *American Literary Anecdotes* (New York: Facts On File, 1990), 227.
2. Alexander Schmemann, *The Historical Road of Eastern Orthodoxy* (Crestwood, New York: St. Vladimir's Seminary Press, 1977), 203.
3. Bainton, *Church,* 66.
4. Dowley, *Eerdman's,* 359.
5. J. N. D. Kelly, *The Oxford Dictionary of Popes* (New York: Oxford University Press, 1986), 258.
6. Durant, *Reformation,* 924.

Chapter 19: Key Figures: Medieval Church Period

1. Furman Bisher, "Blanket of roses for a 92-year-old-rose," *The Atlanta Journal/The Atlanta Constitution*, 6 May 1990, E1.
2. Shelley, *Church*, 203.
3. Osbeck, *101*, 218.
4. Francis of Assisi, *Bartlett's Familiar Quotations* (Boston: Little, Brown and Company, 1980), 138.
5. Shelley, *Church*, 257.
6. Ochino, as quoted by Durant, *Reformation*, 476.

Chapter 20: Writers/Writings: Medieval Church Period

1. Schaff, *History*, vol. IV, 228.
2. John D. Woodbridge, ed., *Great Leaders of the Christian Church* (Chicago: Moody Press, 1988), 110.
3. Urban II, as quoted by Durant, *Age*, 587.
4. *Divine Comedy*, as quoted by Durant, *Age*, 1067.
5. Thomas a Kempis, *The Imitation of Christ* (New York: Doubleday, 1955), 63.

Chapter 21: Trends: Medieval Church Period

1. Fadiman, *Little*, 486.
2. Comby, *How*, 152.
3. Comby, *How*, 146.
4. Filarete, as quoted by Will Durant, *The Renaissance* (New York: Simon and Schuster, 1953), 87.
5. Durant, *Reformation*, 770.
6. Erasmus, as quoted by Durant, *Reformation*, 780.
7. Luther, as quoted by Durant, *Reformation*, 778.

Chapter 23: Story Line: Denominational Church Era

1. Frank Deford, "Sports in China," *Sports Illustrated* (15 August 1988), 38.

Chapter 24: Story Line: Global Church Era

1. John Carey, ed., *Eyewitness to History* (New York: Avon, 1987), 295–8.

Chapter 25: Headlines: Modern Church Period

1. Carey, *Eyewitness,* 242–3.
2. Ruth A. Tucker, *From Jerusalem To Irian Jaya* (Grand Rapids, Michigan: Academie Books, 1983), 154
3. Ibid., 387–8.
4. Ibid., 418–21.
5. Ibid., 676–7.

Chapter 26: Concepts: Modern Church Period

1. Adapted from *Aesop's Fables.*
2. Earle E. Cairns, *Christianity Through the Centuries* (Grand Rapids, Michigan: Zondervan Publishing House, 1981), 339.

Chapter 27: Foes: Modern Church Period

1. Fadiman, *Little,* 360.
2. Voltaire, *Bartlett's,* 344.
3. Dowley, *Eerdman's,* 602.

Chapter 28: Key Figures: Modern Church Period

1. Carey, *Eyewitness,* 223–4.
2. J. D. Douglas, *The New International Dictionary of the Christian Church,* (Grand Rapids, Michigan: Zondervan Publishing House, 1978), 652.
3. Woodbridge, *Great,* 293.
4. John Wesley, "Rule for Christian Living," *Christian History* (February 1983): 6.
5. Dowley, *Eerdman's,* 439.
6. Dowley, *Eerdman's,* 441.
7. Woodbridge, *Great,* 368.
8. Lewis A. Drummond, "The Secrets of Spurgeon's Preaching," *Christian History* (February 1991): 15.
9. Woodbridge, *Great,* 342.

Chapter 29: Writers/Writings: Modern Church Period

1. Hendrickson, *American,* 44.
2. James I, as quoted by Will Durant, *The Age of Reason Begins* (New York: Simon and Schuster, 1961), 152.

3. "Publication of the King James Bible," *Christian History* (November 1990): 44.
4. Marshall Morgan and Scott, *Dangerous Journey* (Grand Rapids, Michigan: Wm. B. Eerdman's Publishing Company, 1985), 7–8.
5. C. S. Lewis, *The Screwtape Letters* (New York: Bantam, 1982), 36.
6. Woodbridge, *Great*, 308.
7. Ibid., 364.

Chapter 30: Trends: Modern Church Period

1. William Meredith, *Partial Accounts* (New York: Alfred A. Knopf, 1987), 85.
2. Ruth A. Tucker, *From Jerusalem to Irian Jaya* (Grand Rapids, Michigan: Zondervan Publishing House, 1983), 357.
3. *International Children's Bible* (Texas: Sweet Publishing, 1986), 634–5.
4. "A Bible made for easy listening," *The Atlanta Journal/The Atlanta Constitution*, 11 May 1991, E7.

INDEX

ABOUT THE AUTHORS

MAX E. ANDERS is Senior Pastor of Grace Covenant Church in Austin, Texas. He is a graduate of Dallas Theological Seminary (Th.M.) and Western Seminary (D.Min.), has taught on the college and seminary level, and ministered with Walk Thru the Bible Ministries before pastoring.

Dr. Anders is listed in "Who's Who Among Young American Professionals" and has been named Outstanding Alumnus of the Year of Grace College, Winona Lake, Indiana. He is the co-author of *Scripture Talks with God* (Nelson), and author of *QuieTimes* (Wolgemuth & Hyatt), *30 Days to Understanding the Bible* (Wolgemuth & Hyatt), and *30 Days to Understanding the Christian Life* (Wolgemuth & Hyatt).

JUDITH A. LUNSFORD graduated from the University of Illinois. In addition to working for the Atomic Energy Commission at the Lawrence Radiation Laboratory in Berkeley, California, she has taught history and literature in secondary schools in the Midwest and the South.

Mrs. Lunsford is the author of *Test Your Christian Literacy* (Wolgemuth & Hyatt). She currently lives in Marietta, Georgia.

The typeface for the text of this book is *Baskerville*. It's creator, John Baskerville (1706-1775), broke with tradition to reflect in his type the rounder, yet more sharply cut lettering of eighteenth-century stone inscriptions and copy books. The type foreshadows modern design in such novel characteristics as the increase in contrast between thick and thin strokes and the shifting of stress from the diagonal to the vertical strokes. Realizing that this new style of letter would be most effective if cleanly printed on smooth paper with genuinely black ink, he built his own presses, developed a method of hot pressing the printed sheet to a smooth, glossy finish, and experimented with special inks. However, Baskerville did not enter into general commercial use in England until 1923.

Substantive Editing:
Michael S. Hyatt

Copy Editing:
Susan Kirby

Cover Design:
Steve Diggs & Friends
Nashville, Tennessee

Page Composition:
Xerox Ventura Publisher
Linotronic L-100 Postscript® Imagesetter

Printing and Binding:
Maple-Vail Book Manufacturing Group,
York, Pennsylvania

Cover Printing:
Strine Printing Company
York, Pennsylvania